W0017632

Only When I Dance

by

Rhoda Demchak

Copyright 2021

All rights reserved. This book or any portion thereof may not be reproduced or
used in any manner whatsoever without the express written permission of the
publisher except for the use of brief quotations in a book review.

ISBN: 978-1-09838-606-1 (print)
ISBN: 978-1-09838-607-8 (eBook)

PREFACE

MY primary intention in writing this book was to honor three women, Mildred Mcintosh, Lula Craig and Mildred Henderson. Every account is based on true occurrences. Many taken from their own journals, diaries and from my own firsthand knowledge.

First purpose in accumulating the events was an effort to leave a written account of these women's lives for future generations.

Second was to help others understand the perspective of these widowed women living in a northern mill town from the 1840s to the 1980s. How they overcame hardships and devastating adversities while continuing to pursue the raising of their children was quite remarkable.

CHAPTER ONE

Goodbye Mama

RETURNING to Mama's room in the ICU, a cold chill slowly proceeded down my spine. I met a young nurse assigned to watch over Mama for the night. Mama had spent 5 days in a coma. The day nurse told me although in a coma Mama probably could hear me.

She could feel my touch. I held her hand and watched as she started to slip away. My mind recalled the milestones we had shared together. High school graduation, my wedding day and the birth of her grandchildren. Ironically, a few months before she became ill, Mama had expressed to me, if she were given a choice, she would never agree to be on life support.

Now, here she was, hooked up to machines that kept her heart beating, her kidneys functioning and a machine allowing her to breathe. If she were able to talk her words would surely be, Damn it, I don't want this!" Earlier, I had received a phone call at the ICU nurse's station from Mama's doctor. He frankly said to me, Mama was never going to get any better. I had a decision to make. He told me if she were his mother, he would take her off life support. In my mind I knew he was right, in my heart I struggled to make that judgement. The conflict was between my heart and mind. From the young age of 2 years old Mama had raised me on her own.

Just the two of us for over twenty years. She was the decision maker in my life. Guiding and informing her judgements about my life. Today the roles had been unexpectedly reversed. A control I had not asked for, nor aspired to. No siblings, no father to support me or rebuke my options. Options ? It was clear there was only one option to choose. Mama's major organs were progressively shutting down each second I delayed.

The night nurse began speaking to me. She interrupted my thoughts about the difficult decision I had made to let Mama go ! She asked if I wanted her to explain the process involved in disconnecting Mama's life support system. A nod was all I could gather together. We wept together as she spoke. Her eyes fixed upon the thin white thermal blanket covering Mama's body. She assured me it would be painless and peaceful for Mama. Mama would simply drift into a deep sleep. The young nurse's voice quivered as she went on. She stumbled over the words having to repeat herself. A part of me felt like she was sharing in my pain and agony. It was past eight when I left the hospital that evening. evening. The staff did not give me an option to stay next to Mama's bed. In my mind, I could hear Mama telling me to go home and be with my family. Mentally drained and six months pregnant were all factors that effected a very emotional drive home.

Even though I was exhausted, sleep did not come easily. Early the next morning I called the ICU at the hospital, as I had done every day Mama was there. The head day nurse told me they had begun removing Mama from life support. She was given pain medication intravenously to ease the transition and was resting comfortably. A time frame was discussed but they did not know how long she may linger.

Pregnant, exhausted and still in denial about the situation, I asked the ICU staff to keep me updated on Mama's condition. Deciding what time to go for the last goodbye was excruciating for me. The staff told me it was unclear when her condition may possibly change. John and I spent much of that Autumn morning outside with our girl. We tried to keep them and ourselves distracted from the impending loss.

After lunch I took a nap, believing I would go to the hospital in the afternoon. When I woke from my nap, I glanced at my wristwatch. The second hand was not moving. It had stopped running at 2:40 p.m. It was now 2:57 pm. As I was wondering whether to leave for the hospital by myself, or take the girls to John's parents and have him drive me to Portland, my thoughts were disrupted by the loud ringing of our phone.

Sadly, it was the ICU nurse informing me that Mama had peacefully passed away a few minutes ago. Just like that ! I had not made it back to say goodbye !

A fact that has haunted me ever since. Upon receiving the news of Mama's death, I asked the nurse on the phone what time she passed. I was shocked to hear her say 2:40 pm was the exact time Mama took her last breath. Orphaned at 31. A strange feeling overcame me like I was the last one. For decades listening to stories from Mama and Nana about those in our family who survived tragedies, pursued dreams with resilience and endurance. Who would I ask for guidance or sustenance now ? So many women before me had wrongly or rightly presented which path to take. Who would tell their stories to our descendants going forth?

The birth of a third daughter prompted me to gather together the diaries, journals and firsthand accounts depicting the lives of these women who came before. Here are their stories.

CHAPTER TWO

AMANDA

AMANDA Newell was born in July 1844 in Litchfield, Maine. She met and married her first husband Joel Small at the age of 18. Joel was a 23 year old farmer in Bowdoin, Maine. Young and feisty, Amanda soon learned the hard truth of farm life. Working from sun up to sun down in the crop fields and caring for a barnyard of animals kept Joel extremely busy. When at nineteen Amanda gave birth to her first child Lillian, her separation anxiety from her parents became less prevalent. A year later Franklin was born followed by Marcha, Viletia, George, Robert, John, Mildred and Amanda. Nine children filled the Small household before Amanda had turned 34 years of age.

Amanda ultimately became disheartened with the farm lifestyle. In her mid -thirties, she fled the farm life and her family. Amanda abandoned her husband and nine children in search of a new freedom with another man. Eventually she married the other man, Colby Bean when she was 46. Amanda had a son with Bean.

The family remained bitter towards Amanda for many years. Her children with Joel lost all communication with her. They financially struggled while trying to help each other through the hardships.

Years later, when her children were all grown with their own families, Amanda came back into their lives. She was frail now. Amanda was without a permanent residence. Her grandchildren called her Gram Bean.

During the final years of her life, Amanda rotated at the homes of her children. A month living with one, two months with another. Her daughter Mildred became Amanda's most frequent caretaker.

Mildred kept a rocking chair in the center of her kitchen for Amanda to rock in. With her hair pulled up in a tight bun high upon her head, Amanda would rock for hours in that rocking chair.

Amanda smoked a corn cob pipe as she rocked. A smoking habit Mildred detested but nonetheless endured, to keep the peace. Mildred had wanted her own children and grandchildren to know Amanda or Gram Bean. Mildred herself wanted to learn things about her mother. Insights or perceptions she had been deprived of in her own childhood. I do not know if Mildred ever truly forgave Amanda for abandoning the family. Perhaps Mildred allowed herself to understand the circumstances.

When Amanda died at the age of 89, it was her once abandoned children who stepped forward to pay for her funeral and burial in Bowdoin.

CHAPTER THREE

MILDRED SMALL MCINTOSH

HEARING stories about Mildred Small Mcintosh really fascinated me. She was revealed as being both physically and mentally strong. Adjectives like resilient, spirited and gutsy were often used to describe her. When Amanda deserted her husband and nine children, young Mildred stepped up to help father Joel manage his large brood. Joel's valiant efforts to keep his family together, work the farm and move forward was often overshadowed by fatigue and a loss of patience.

The strain allowed for tempers to flare sometimes in the crowded Small family household. Mildred's strong will was enhanced by her rebellious spirit giving great challenge to her father. At fourteen, Mildred found it difficult to hope for a future aside from a substitute mother to her eight siblings and working tirelessly on the farm. She harbored dreams about her two passions.

A passion for horses and a passion to gain freedom from the farm. The two passions evolved and ultimately changed her future. Mildred met a charming older man named, I. Lester Mcintosh. He was the proprietor of the local livery stable. Mcintosh was also a successful merchant who owned and operated retail businesses in the town.

The ambitious Mcintosh truly enjoyed Mildred's obvious adoration. Even though he was eleven years her senior and previously wed, (records are unclear if he was divorced or widowed), Mcintosh began to aggressively court the teenage girl.

Mcintosh told Mildred her maturity with family responsibilities combined with her youthful manner were qualities he needed to help him achieve his future goals.

Mcintosh's attention towards Mildred made her feel special. For the first time in her life Mildred felt like she was a priority to someone.

After a rather short courtship, twenty-seven year old I. Lester Mcintosh and sixteen year old Mildred Small were married. Mildred moved into Mcintosh's two-story dwelling on corner of Main street in Lisbon Falls. The large house stood adjacent to Mcintosh's livery stable where they had first met. Mildred was fascinated with the town lifestyle. She found it distinctively different from her life growing up on the farm. A successful merchant in the town, Mcintosh's businesses consumed the majority of his time. Children soon dominated Mildred's time and her life.

Daughter May was born within the first year of their marriage. Next came Irving, Helen, Lula, Zorena, Margaret, Robert and Abner each exactly two years apart. Sadly, in 1990 Mildred suffered a stillborn birth.

Her growing family kept her extremely busy. Mcintosh spent many hours maintaining and operating his several business endeavors. As the years progressed Mcintosh had less and less time for Mildred and the children. His livery stable and mercantile stores were flourishing.

The name Mcintosh became quite familiar in the rapidly growing town of Lisbon Falls. In the fall of 1911 a campaign, promoting Mcintosh apples at a local orchard, awarded the large Mcintosh family a bushel of their Mcintosh apples.

A local newspaper sent a photographer to cover the newsworthy event. The young red-haired man, nicknamed "Moon" because of his large round face, became very fond of Mildred and her children.

"Moon" enjoyed photographing the large Mcintosh brood. On hot summer days after a photo session, he would treat Mildred to a fountain drink at a nearby drugstore. Her favorite drinks were root beer floats or sarsaparillas.

In 1912 Mildred became pregnant once again. Vedah Louise Mcintosh was born with bright red hair. I. Lester Mcintosh was thrilled. He said he had always wanted a child with red hair.

Unfortunately, Mcintosh's time with his youngest child was short-lived. He succumbed to heart failure when Vedah was only nine months old. People believed his heavy work load and stress led to Mcintosh's death.

The bulk of Mcintosh's estate was specified by the courts to go primarily to his children. Mildred retained the house to raise the children but was instructed by a judge to keep a detailed ledger for all expenditures regarding the Mcintosh children's welfare. Everything purchased right down to a pair of shoelaces, had to be logged in the ledger to justify each dollar spent.

Mildred Small Mcintosh became a widow at 36, with nine children to raise alone. The family of ten decided as each Mcintosh child turned 21 years of age, they would agree to sign over any remaining estate money for Mildred to live on. Eldest daughter May refused at first to relent her inheritance at twenty-one, until much persuasion by her siblings changed her mind.

The estate was nearly depleted by the time Vedah turned twenty-one years of age. Living in a mill town meant Mildred's brood each worked in the mill at one time or another. The Worumbo woolen mill was named after the Kennebec Indians tribal Chief Worumbo.

Operated by Mr. Gutman, the woolen product made at Worumbo was said to be one of the finest woolens made in the entire country. The Worumbo's quality woolens were well suited for the U.S. Navy. They ordered the blue dyed woolens for all of their blue Navy uniforms.

The woolen mill stood less than 100 yards from Mildred Mcintosh's front door. May was first to work in the mill. She left after a short time and traveled to Boston, Massachusetts to work.

While working in Boston May met an Italian man named, Theodore Ricci. They soon married and had one son she met an Italian man named, Theodore Ricci. They soon married and had one son, Theodore Ricci Jr. Everyone in our family nicknamed their son Ted.

I remember May as being small and petite. Her stature a mere 4 feet 10 inches tall. We heard many in the family called her prudent or tight. This a contrast to the fact that her siblings were generous to a fault. They were especially generous with giving food to others. A family anecdote was, every Christmas, May would give each family unit a single pint of her homemade spaghetti sauce. The recipe had come from her husband's family. It didn't matter if a family unit consisted of two or ten, she never gave them more than one pint.

Oldest son Irving worked part-time as a clerk in the Lisbon Falls post office while in high school. He later worked for a couple years at the nearby Pejepscot paper mill. He ultimately came back to the post office earning a permanent position as US postmaster.

Irving was postmaster for over 30 years. He married a local girl named Frances Beals. She played organ at the Episcopal church on main street in Lisbon Falls. Together they raised seven children in a house next door to the church.

My memories of Uncle Irving include his love of family and his dry sense of humor. He liked to tell corny jokes to us youngsters often embarrassing his own children in the process.

Next came Helen, she passed away before I was born. I understand she married but never had children. Born in 1900 was my grandmother Lula next in the birth line. Zorena, who we called Rena was born next. She became the first girl in the family to graduate high school go on to receive a teaching degree. Rena married a farmer and had a daughter.

What I remember about Aunt Rena were her large vegetable gardens. Each fall at harvest time she generously gave family members bushels of fresh vegetables. These bushels of vegetables happily fed and nourished us through those long Maine winters. Thank you, Aunt Rena.

A sister Margaret came next. She met husband Carl Penley at the woolen mill. The Penleys lived on a farm a few miles out of town. Their only child, Royal was mentally handicapped. He never reached a mental capacity beyond three years of age. His parents refused to put Royal in an institution. He basically spent his days watching television or filling in coloring books.

My cousins and I loved playing on Carl's farm. A few days each summer, we would go to the farm in the morning and come home before dark. Some days at the farm we played hide and seek with Royal or simply chase each other all around the wide open hayfields.

There was a narrow grassy path between Margaret and Carl's farm and her brother Abner's summer cabin. By the end of those summer days, we cousins had worn the grassy path down to bare dirt.

CHAPTER FOUR

Robert

SON Robert, known as Bob, was considered the black sheep of the family. I understand his siblings were never in trouble with the law. Not Bob. He had a major drinking problem. His drinking became an issue early on in his life. Bob also loved to drive fast. The fast driving is why bootleggers and rum runners became his friends and accomplices.

During the prohibition years bootleggers wanted someone young as their driver. It was thought law enforcement would not suspect Bob. After all he came from a respected, hometown, law abiding family. The bootleggers gave Bob cash and free booze to transport alcohol from town to town. Bob was pleased about this deal. It did not sit well with mother Mildred. His mother hated anything to do with booze.

Until Bob, she had been successful in raising her children to stay clear of it. Bob a teen, had been smuggling alcohol for quite some time before Mildred discovered what he was doing. One time Bob's cronies decided to hide their crates of booze at his house because the cops were getting too close to them. Bob happily agreed.

Mildred preferred doing her housework in the evening when her family had gone to bed. She would often carry a pot of burning incense throughout the house to destroy bad odors. One evening as she finished cleansing the house, she found an unfamiliar crate hidden behind the kitchen door. Mildred opened the mystery crate.

She was horrified to find it filled with rum and whiskey bottles. Mildred was furious. She took the bottles from the crate and began pouring the contents down the kitchen sink drain.

Bob heard a sound like water running in the kitchen and decided to investigate. He was outraged to find his mother emptying the contents of the whiskey and rum bottles. A trait both Bob and Mildred shared was a quick temper. He began screaming at his mother to stop. Bob even lunged at her, with his hand raised as if he were going to strike her. His six foot 140 pound frame was quite a contrast to his mother Mildred. She barely stood five feet tall and tipped the scales at over 300 pounds. Whether she felt threatened or was just angry, Mildred grabbed a nearby axe and swung it towards her son.

Bob immediately backed off. She warned him if he ever brought booze into her home again, she would kill him. Bob promised never to bring booze home again. Family members insisted that even though Bob caused her problems, he was Mildred's favorite.

Perhaps Mildred favored Bob because she saw him as a challenge. Maybe she refused to accept his failures. No matter how many times provoked, the mother factor never wavered. A point proven when Bob was actually arrested for driving for the bootleggers. Mildred had to bring him to appear before a judge in court. Amidst great resistance by the teenager, she forced Bob to wear short pants with suspenders, high socks and a white buttoned up shirt. Her effort to convince the judge that Bob was younger and too immature to understand his misconduct worked. Bob stayed out of jail.

Unfortunately, Bob's heavy drinking never really ceased after those incidents. He did try to stay out of trouble. Like his siblings, he went to work at the Worumbo woolen mill. It was at the mill where he met a young woman named Ethel. She was very shy and withdrawn. Bob could be charming He had acquired his mother's culinary talents. Ethel was impressed. Tragically, she had been raised in an abusive home. Ethel had experienced both physical and sexual abuse as a child. Bob was her escape.

They married and had two sons born 12 years apart. The second childbirth was life-threatening for Ethel. Her health issues and Bob's continuing excessive drinking eventually ended the marriage. Even after the divorce they seemed to care about one another. Many years later, my mother and I lived in an apartment above Bob's. I remember great smells coming from his kitchen as he prepared one of his favorite dishes.

CHAPTER FIVE

VEDAH

VEDAH was the youngest of Mildred's brood. Her two oldest siblings had already moved out on their own by the time she was born. Vedah and six others remained at home. Mildred continued to work in the candy store adjacent to her home to bring in extra money. Lula enjoyed spending time with her baby sister. She even took Vedah along on dates with her husband to be Melbourne. Vedah loved the attention from Lula and Melbourne. After they wed, she often stayed at their home across the river in Durham. When Lula came over to pick up Vedah one morning, Mildred told Lula the doctor had been called. Vedah was very ill. She had stopped eating and was running a fiver. The doctor examined the child thoroughly. He could not explain the cause of her illness. For several days, Vedah's condition deteriorated. Finally, the doctor came to the conclusion she had parasites and may not survive.

Mildred was heartbroken. She watched as her little girl became lethargic and weak. Lula insisted something could be done. She asked her mother if Vedah could come stay with her. Mildred said she could not bear to watch her child die. She agreed to let Lula take Vedah. Lula had heard about an Indian woman who lived near the riverbank. She knew the Indian woman sold unusual types of tonics to treat many ailments. Lula took Vedah to see the Indian woman. As soon as the Indian woman saw the child, she knew exactly the remedy to rid her of the parasites.

The Indian woman told Lula she had recently skinned a skunk and had saved the grease or fat from it. She gave Lula a jar of the skunk grease. Lula was told to spread the skunk grease on bread and feed it to Vedah. Lula resisted the suggestion at first. The Indian woman claimed it could save Vedah's life. Considering this to be a last effort to save her, Lula agreed to the remedy. Each day for three weeks, Lula spread a small amount of skunk grease on bread and forced Vedah to eat it. Within a couple of days Vedah began passing large worms from her body. As more worms emerged her health amazingly began to greatly improve. She was less lethargic and had an increased appetite. A month after these treatments Vedah was back to her normal self. The doctor was astonished. Vedah returned home to a truly grateful Mildred. Vedah was energetic, social and always the life of the party. In her teen years, Mildred would constantly reprimand her for making dates with more than one suitor on the same night. One night Vedah asked her mother to tell Charlie, who was ringing the doorbell that she was sick or gone. Vedah ran out the back door with another young man.

The situation was uncomfortable for Mildred because she actually preferred Charlie. He was quiet, well-mannered and respectful. In contrast the backdoor fellow was, in Mildred's words, a wild guy.

Nonetheless, Mildred went to the front door to speak to Charlie. When he asked if Vedah was ready, she truthfully told him she had no idea where Vedah was at the time. The answer was true since Vedah took off out the back door and never said where she was going.

Vedah the social butterfly decided that she did not like her given name. She went to court and had it legally changed to Verda instead. I have very fond memories of Aunt Verda.

Although not a familiar disorder in the 1960's, I believe Verda had OCD. She was extremely clean even rewashing her clean laundry if it sat for more than a day in her laundry basket. Verda was a people person too. Many described her as having the gift of gab. She loved to talk. She seemed to be a member of every women's social organization in the state. Verda was a wonderful cook. She would offer food to anyone and everyone who entered her home.

Her favorite pastime was to browse through all the cookbooks in her home. During WWII she met and married a young serviceman named

Mike. They raised two children together. For most of her life she worked in retail a place where she could happily interact with the public.

Verda was diagnosed with MS in her fifties. MS eventually confined her to a wheelchair and sent her to reside in a nursing home. Her mobility take away, Verda still managed to become the social director and activities coordinator of the facility.

Abner was the youngest son. He was interested in finance and real estate. After high school Abner enlisted in the Army. He later transferred to the Air Force. During this time, he became stricken with polio.

His family was notified that due to his illness Abner would have an early discharge. Weeks of hospitalization followed before coming home to be cared for by his mother Mildred.

Abner's weight loss from polio meant his sisters and mother were able to carry him to and from his bed. It took a long time for him to regain his strength back. Once recovered Abner became a successful accountant. He was a selectman on the Lisbon Falls town council. Abner became a landlord after purchasing several apartment buildings in the town. He was in his forties when Rosemond, a registered nurse, became his wife. Although Abner and Rosemond did not have children of their own, they provided a loving home for Abner's great niece.

On summer days, we cousins enjoyed visiting his small cabin next to Margaret's farm. We cousins had hours of adventurous fun in the small section of woods surrounding the cabin.

CHAPTER SIX

Lula McIntosh Craig

LULA Hazel Mcintosh was Mildred and Lester's fourth child and third daughter. As I stated earlier, she was my grandmother, my Nana. Lula enjoyed cooking, sewing and caring for her siblings. Twelve years of age when her father died mother Mildred decided she needed Lula at home to help with the large family. Lula never went beyond the 8th grade in school. While her siblings liked working in the Worumbo woolen mill, Lula preferred housekeeping jobs to earn a living.

In the summer months, wealthy people from out of state rented cottages on the islands along Maine's coastline. Lula traveled by horse and buggy to Harpswell, Orrs Island and Bailey Island to work as housekeeper, cook and child care provider. In the winter months, she often cleaned and cooked for some of the doctors who lived in Lisbon Falls.

After I. Lester's death, his retail businesses were sold but the livery stable next to the Mcintosh home remained. People would ride the train from Boston or New York into Lisbon Falls. These travelers hired horses, wagons or buggies from Mcintosh's livery stable. Mcintosh had used the services of a Durham blacksmith named Silas Craig for years.

Growing up, Lula had interacted with the Craig children when they visited Silas at the livery stable. Lula especially liked the eldest son, Melbourne Craig. Lula called Mel (his nickname) lanky, because he stood 6 feet 4 and was rail thin. She found Mel quite handsome, charming with a dry sense of humor.

Mel would tease Lula about being older than he was, by six months. My Nana was barely 5 feet tall with a stout build which made them an unusual looking pair. When Lula turned 16 she began dating Mel Craig.

The Craig family lived three miles from Lisbon Falls across the railroad tracks in the town of Durham.

Silas had a blacksmith shop in the barn next to their farmhouse. His wife Delilah kept busy raising her five sons and two daughters. She preferred to be called Lila instead of her given name because as a deeply religious woman, Lila did not want to be perceived as the bad woman in the bible named Delilah.

The Craig family were devoted members of Shiloh Kingdom church in Durham. During this period the church's history was surrounded by controversy even considered a cult. Melbourne left Shiloh church after church leaders stated he was to marry whom they had selected. He became a charter member of the Nazarene church in Lisbon Falls

Playing harmonica, guitar and singing was a passionate interest of Melbourne's. His deep baritone voice was welcomed into several choral groups like the Men of Song and Litchfield Songsters.

Lula shared Melbourne's love of music as well. She played the piano and church organ on occasion. Lula was a member of the First Congregational Church where Melbourne's choral groups sometimes performed.

Mel gave Lula horse and buggy rides, to and from her housekeeping jobs down to the islands. These 4 hour commutes helped transform their friendship into love. Lula and Melbourne became engaged at seventeen. He became head electrician at the Worumbo woolen mill.

They started saving money for the nuptials. On September 18th 1920, Lula Mcintosh and Melbourne Craig were wed. The couple moved into a small rented house in Durham, less than 5 miles from their childhood homes. Exactly nine months later, a baby girl was born to them. Lula named her Mildred Louise for her mother and her favorite aunt. Mildred's birth transformed Lula's mother into Gram Mac.

Lula had become good friends with her closest neighbor Mrs. Beals. Mrs. Beals lived on a hill about 900 feet beyond Lula's house. Mrs. Beals loved babies and was overjoyed at having one nearby. She was a widow with one grown son Olin. He was much older than Lula. Olin's personality was profoundly different than Mrs. Beals.

She was kindhearted and caring. Olin was extremely self-centered and cold-hearted. Mrs. Beals shared a story with Lula about Olin. He had sent for a mail-order bride ten years before. When the young girl departed the train to greet him, Olin noticed she had a club foot. He immediately told the girl to leave on the next train. Olin stated he wanted an unblemished or perfect wife not a cripple ! He never married.

Lula felt assured she had enough childcare experience to handle anything that arose with her new baby girl. After all, she had helped raise five younger siblings. Regrettably, her knowledge was challenged during a harsh winter snowstorm when baby Mildred was 8 months old. Winter storms in Maine can be very brutal. The temperatures often dip well below freezing especially when high winds are a factor.

Lula tried to keep the wood stove stoked because the old house was extremely drafty. She lay the baby down in the cradle Melbourne had made, while she went to gather more firewood from the frozen woodpile behind the house.

Even with multiple layers of clothing, Lula could still feel the bitter cold wind on her skin. Her arms loaded with snow covered firewood, Lula slowly made her way back inside the house.

After placing firewood on the grate next to the stove, Lula pulled off her boots and snowy clothes. She hung them near the fire to dry. Lula walked over to check on her sleeping baby girl. As she laid her hand upon the baby's chest Lula was shocked to find it still.

Scooping the motionless Mildred into her arms, Lula listened for breathing sounds. Silence ! She hurriedly wrapped the baby in blankets, put her cold wet clothes back on and ran out the door. Lula's visibility was hampered by the falling snow. She forged toward the house on the hill. Feeling like she was moving in slow motion, Lula plowed a path with her feet up to Mrs. Beals house. When she reached Mrs. Beals house Lula almost passed out from exhaustion. Thankfully Mrs. Beals saw her as she neared the door.

Lula feared she lacked the strength to pound on the door. Once inside she cried out that her baby was not breathing. Mrs. Beals grabbed the baby from Lula and immediately undressed her.

She told Olin to fetch the doctor with their horse and wagon. Mrs. Beals put cool water over the baby's hot body. Within a minute or two the baby started to respond and wake up. Lula had heard about fever convulsions but had never actually seen a baby have one.

Mrs. Beals told her that sometimes if a child gets too hot they can have a seizure and stop breathing. By the time the doctor had arrived baby Mildred was doing fine. Fortunately, Mildred never experienced anymore fever seizures or convulsions. None of Lula's future children were subject to the condition either.

A second daughter, Idolyne was born three years later. Her name came from a long weekend trip Melbourne and Lula took to New Hampshire during her second pregnancy.

They had driven passed a motel named the " Idyl Inn ". Lula liked the name for a girl. A boy would surely be named after Mel. My Nana repeated this story each and every time our family made the annual fall foliage trip to New Hampshire.

Now that her family was growing, Lula decided they needed a larger home. Perhaps more land for a vegetable garden and some farm animals. They moved a quarter mile, down the road, to a larger L-shaped farmhouse with a barn and garage.

By this time automobiles were becoming very popular and affordable. Mel bought a used Model A for his family. Lula began planting vegetables in her new garden. She used printed grain bags to make clothes for her and the children. With the left over strips of cloth Lula braided them into rugs for the house.

Lula felt having children 4-5 years apart was working out well. When Idolyne was 5 years old another sibling was born into the Craig family. A boy was born in 1930. He was named Melbourne Stanley Craig but not a junior because Mel's middle name was Frederick.

Everyone in the family called him Stanley as not to confuse him with his father. Being quite stout and having a short torso created very difficult births for Lula. Ten pound Stanley was particularly hard. All her deliveries were at a birthing house in Lisbon Falls. Sometimes the doctor arrived on time, other times a midwife delivered the child. Lula herself had often helped as a midwife working alongside the town doctor.

Eldest Mildred would stay with Gram Mcintosh, while little sister Idolyne, was sent to stay at Grammie Craig's house, when Lula gave birth. Mel adored his daughters but was delighted to have a son to share his love of automobiles.

Grammie Craig, having had five sons, told Lula to be prepared for many years of soiled greasy clothes from working on automobiles.

When Stanley was only three years of age Mel found an old pedal car to restore for him. He gave it one new feature a car battery was placed in the rear and wired to the pedal.

Mel made the battery powered car a surprise for Stanley. He brought the altered pedal car to the local hardware store in Lisbon Falls. Mel asked the owner if he would place it in the store front window for a few days. The owner agreed. The very next Sunday after church, Mel took young Stanley for a walk passed the hardware store.

Of course when Stanley saw the fancy pedal car, he asked to have it. Mel gave him a long lecture about having to behave and obey his mother before the pedal car could come home with them. Stanley promised he would never be bad again if he could only have that pedal car.

Mel had never deceived anyone in his life and could not continue the teasing. He quickly told Stanley he had indeed made the pedal car for him. Stanley drove that car for hours each and every day. One story Nana told was how Stanley drove the car into a large mud puddle. He was really stuck in the mud.

Amidst flying mud everywhere Stanley kept his foot on the pedal until the battery was drained and dead. Lula and Mel were watching the entire episode from their kitchen window. Mel was smiling and obviously enjoying his son's antics. Lula on the other hand failed to see the humor and she believed he should be punished once he came out of that mud puddle.

Grammie Craig was correct about those Craig genes. Stanley would spend hours in their garage watching Mel work on cars. One time Mel took an automobile completely apart and rebuilt it only to discover several extra parts left on the garage floor. It didn't seem to matter. The car drove just fine.

Stanley in fact was known to begin changing car tires at age 4. He started driving the family car at five years of age. Yes, that is true ! Many family members told the story about when Mel brought home a newly purchased 1935 Dodge for the family. Lula had been anxiously waiting to see the new automobile. When Mel came into the house, Lula looked out the doorway to see the new car. There was no new car to be seen.

She asked where the car was. Mel calmly told her that he let five year old Stanley drive it to the back fields. Lula was not pleased.

Ten minutes later, they watched young Stanley come into view driving the new car. He was teetering on the edge of the front seat in order to reach the clutch, brake and gas pedals. Stanley's head barely visible above the steering wheel.

He was grinning from ear to ear as he drove that brand new Dodge automobile. Lula knew she was fighting a losing battle.

In the years that followed Stanley's love of automobiles only grew deeper.

Lula, like her mother Mildred, was pleasingly plump. Her siblings teased her by saying Lula was 5 foot high and just as wide. In fact Lula's heaviness hid her pregnancies. One day two inquisitive sisters, Mildred age

14 and 10 year old Idolyne were snooping around in their parents' bedroom. They opened Lula's wooden trunk and discovered a pile of newly sewn baby clothes. The girls were puzzled. At age 36 they considered their mother too old to have another baby.

Whether planned or not, Mel told his children that night it was true. A week later the labor pains began. Lula was taken to the birthing house in Lisbon Falls. Mildred again went to stay at Gram Mcintosh's house. Idolyne and Stanley were sent to Grammie Craig's house. Sadly, this birth was a tragic one. The baby, another boy, was born with hydrocephalus. More commonly called water on the brain.

Lula was physically exhausted and mentally depressed after the birth. Mel asked family members to keep the children a couple of weeks longer to give Lula more time to heal. Mel told the children the very sad news when they came home. It was difficult for them to understand. Lula named the baby boy Lester, after her father. He was buried on the Mcintosh family burial lot in Lisbon Falls next to her father. Lula never got pregnant again.

A few years later, Mel and Lula decided to move again. This time into a four bedroom, two story house about 1800 feet down the road. The house did not have a lot of acreage and was less than 100 feet from the main road. The Craig children were now grown and beginning lives of their own. Mildred finished high school and beautician school. She interned at a local hair salon before eventually opening her own salon in Lisbon Falls called, Mildred's Beauty Shop.

CHAPTER SEVEN

CRAIG

IDOLYNE quit high school. She married at eighteen and moved out of town. Lula and Mel's first grandchild was Idolyne's son whom she named Craig. When Craig was 3 years old he started staying weekends with his maternal grandparents. Idolyne now divorced worked in a Lewiston shoe factory. Craig had inherited Mel's sense of humor. Through the years we were told about the "little Craig" stories.

Craig was a precarious youngster. Like the time Idolyne and Craig walked to a local Lewiston drugstore where he took candy without paying for it. When Idolyne discovered what Craig had done she walked him back to the store to return the stolen candy.

On the way back home, she saw a policeman standing in front of their apartment building. Idolyne decided to teach Craig an important lesson. She brought him up to the policeman and loudly told Craig that if he stole again the policeman would punish him.

Three year old Craig looked up at the policeman and said loudly, " I ain't scared of you ! The policeman smiled replying, " I don't want you to be scared of me young man, I'm here to help and protect you."

Idolyne was embarrassed and upset that her plan backfired. Next came the time Craig, still 3, was staying at Mel and Lula's house. Lula placed Craig in a wooden playpen outside on her front lawn about fifty feet from the main road. Craig kept stacking toys up so he could climb out over the playpen and head towards the road.

Mel was home on lunch break. He caught Craig each time, placing him back inside the enclosure. The final time he escaped Mel, who never swore a day in his life or spanked his children, grabbed Craig within a couple feet of the road and lightly tapped him on his bottom.

Craig quickly looked up at his 6 foot 4 inch grandfather and shouted, "what the hell the matter with you ?"

Even though Mel disliked the " hell" usage he turned away to smile at the child's response. Another little Craig incident, often shared with us cousins, when he was four years old he and his mother were again at my grandparents' house when Craig began to misbehave. He kept interrupting Idolyne's conversation with persistent requests for a drink of water. His mother refused him and sent Craig upstairs to one of the bedrooms for punishment. Below the bedroom was the kitchen where his mother and grandparents were talking.

The bedroom had a floor grate which enabled Craig to hear everything they were saying. Obviously they too could hear him yelling about still wanting a drink of water. Idolyne hollered back through the grate for Craig to be quiet. She did this more than once. The las time he yelled down she threatened to come upstairs if he did not be quiet.

Craig quickly replied back to her, " When you come up, could you bring me a drink of water ?" The ironic reality is this mischievous young- ster grew up to be a fine young man. He served four years in the Marine Corps before becoming a Secret Service agent in the White House. Craig honorably served five presidents, Nixon, Ford, Carter, Reagan and George H.W. Bush.

Early in her marriage, Lula became friends with a black woman from the south named Clara. I heard Clara and her daughter Bertha moved north to Maine around the late 1920's or early 1930's. Lula and Clara often swapped stories about when both were housekeepers. Lula had worked for wealthy summer residents on Maine coastal islands before she was mar- ried. Clara related how she had worked on large southern plantations homes as a young child alongside her mother. She remembered long days polishing lots of brass doorknobs until they were bright and shiny. The doorknobs appearance had to pass the plantation owners approval.

Lula was told Clara's first husband, Bertha's father, was an American Indian. Lula first met Clara and Bertha after the mother and daughter had married the two Shaw brothers who lived near her in Durham.

Bertha Shaw and her husband moved into a house approximately 800 ft. behind Lula's house. Neither Bertha nor Lula owned a phone. Every time Bertha became pregnant she had a special way to let Lula know when she was in labor and ready to give birth. Bertha would hang a white towel on her clothesline in direct view of Lula's kitchen window. If Lula looked out her kitchen window and saw the white towel waving on the clothesline, she started walking towards Bertha's house. Bertha's husband would drive to the doctor's to notify him. Several times the doctor did not arrive before the birth. Since Lula often worked as a midwife with the doctor, Bertha felt comfortable having her do the delivery. Bertha gave birth to 12 children. Lula probably delivered half of them. When the moment came to give the baby a name Lula often suggested a name from her own family.

Many of Bertha's children were named after Lula's brothers or sisters. Years later, Bertha moved into the house where Mrs. Beals had lived. Bertha and Lula remained friends their entire lives. Sometimes in the summer, when Nana visited Bertha she would bring my cousin Deb and I with her so we could play with Bertha's grandkids. More than a decade later after both Nana and Bertha had passed away, I was surprised to meet up with Bertha's relatives at a wedding reception. The bride was Bertha's granddaughter and the groom was my husband's cousin. I spoke with two of Bertha's daughters who insisted I resembled Lula. They spoke fondly of my Nana and my mother, who I learned had attended school with them.

We all shared a laugh about how Nana had influenced Bertha's choice of names to included many of her siblings names.

CHAPTER EIGHT

LIFE CHANGES

LULA'S son Stanley was nineteen when he married his 14 year old girl-friend Frances and became a parent. Mel built them a house right next door to his and Lula's. When the baby boy was born he was named Stanley too. Although, he was not a junior because his father's legal name was Melbourne Stanley Craig. He was an adorable little blonde, blue eyed boy who resembled his father. At 14, Stanley's wife was overwhelmed at the prospect of taking care of this little boy Many family members tried to support the young couple by helping to furnish their house, buying them groceries or sewing clothes for the baby. He was the second grandchild and second grandson for Mel and Lula.

Mel helped Stanley get a job at the Worumbo Mill working alongside him. Being very young parents took a toll on them. Some days Stanley failed to show up for work. His young wife liked to spend time with her girlfriends while her parents took care of the baby. Two years later when a second child was born, a daughter named Deborah, the marriage had collapsed. Both seemed to want their freedom.

They mutually agreed to divorce. Deborah was only a few months old when her parents divorced. In court when the custody of the minor children was presented before the judge, Frances told the judge that she and her son would be moving in with her parents. The judge agreed that decision was acceptable due to the fact she was under 18 years of age.

Stanley also stood before the judge. He stated to the court that his parents would take care of the baby girl. Unfortunately, Stanley had failed to ask his parents to do so before making that statement. Mel and Lula were in their early fifties. The prospect of starting over with an infant was a challenge neither had planned on.

Nonetheless, both agreed to raise the baby girl in their home. It was settled. Deborah was to reside with her grandparents, Lula and Melbourne Craig. Under the circumstances it was unclear if Deborah's continuous crying was from colic or feeling abandoned. Daytime hours while Mel worked, Lula did her best to soothe the baby by rocking her. In the evening Mel would cradle the baby girl in his arms and walk the floor for hours to allow Lula to get some rest. Eventually exhausted from crying Deborah would fall asleep. Mel would catch 4-5 hours of sleep before going back to work at the mill.

They both loved and adored Deborah. She became the center of their lives. Lula was fearful about the house being so close to the road. Being older they felt it difficult for them to keep the toddler a safe distance from the nearby road. Deborah was around 4 years old when Mel and Lula decided to move back into the old farmhouse, where they had raised all four of their children. Over 700 feet away from any main road and acres of land for Deborah to play made the decision an easy one.

They could envision her running around the vast fields on the 40 acre farm. Some parts of barn had deteriorated leaving only a small section for Mel to use as storage. Son Stanley had remarried with a new baby. This prompted Mel to give him a section of the property about 900 yards to the right of the farmhouse. Stanley began building a new house for his new family. In the summer of 1955, Mel and Lula began to restore and renovate the old farmhouse before moving in. Each room received a new coat of paint. Floor boards were replaced on the porch. Mel rewired the light fixtures and electrical outlets. Lula braided area rugs for every room plus she braided a set of stair runners.

At 55, Mel and Lula decided this would be the house they'd spend the rest of their lives in. It would be the home Deborah would be raised in. Lula once again plowed the land for a large garden. On the first Friday of September my grandparents moved all but their bedroom furniture into the newly remodeled farmhouse. Lula had cleaned and scrubbed their current residence in preparation for its future occupants.

No one really knew the definite cause. Was it faulty wiring or a lit cigarette? There were cigarette butts found all over the road leading to the farmhouse. Couples often took advantage of the old farmhouse road, during the years it was abandoned,using it for a hang out to drink or smoke.

Whatever the source was, on that Sunday evening, my grandparents dream to live out their lives in that old farmhouse went up in smoke. The entire structure burned to the ground leaving only the cement foundation visible. Mel and Lula were devastated.

At 3 a.m. my parents, Tup and Mildred, were notified by Stanley about the fire. They drove up from Bath, about an hour away, to give support and comfort to my grandparents. A bedroom set and the clothes on their backs was all they had until further plans could be made. Without hesitation, Stanley offered them his incomplete building to live in. He and his family moved into the one surviving structure on the property, the garage. The garage stood between the barn and the burned farmhouse.

Basically, a 14x14 foot structure with two small windows and a sliding wood door. Mel assured Stanley it would be temporary until the farmhouse was rebuilt. Lula never got over that fire. Decades later her eyes still filled with tears when someone mentioned the burned farmhouse. Losing her furniture, clothing and kitchen goods was tough enough but the worse loss for Nana was all her family photographs had been destroyed in the fire.

Years later each time she saw a piece of furniture similar to what she'd had Nana would say" I used to have one like that but I lost it in the fire."

Then Lula would say, " I thank God no one was hurt." Stanley transformed the old garage into a suitable dwelling to live in for the winter. Lula, Mel and young Deborah lived in the new house which was still under construction.

After a cold winter, Mel and Lula looked forward to the Spring as a new beginning for them, saving money to rebuild where the farmhouse had stood.

It seemed life was moving forward for the Craig family. Sadly, on April 11, 1956 tragedy struck Lula's world again. My grandfather was involved in a freak accident at the Worumbo woolen mill. He was using a pressurized nail gun to secure wires near the ceiling in one of the rooms in the woolen mill. Being head electrician, Mel did most of the wiring himself but on this particular day he needed assistance to finish his task. My grandfather asked a young man who worked maintenance at the mill to help him. The young man was labeled " mentally slow" by some but Mel wanted to give him a chance to perhaps learn a trade and prove himself. While Mel stood atop the ten foot ladder he explained each process of the job to the young man. Loading and passing the nail gun to my grandfather became his one and only job.

No one knows if the young man forgot to click the safety latch on or whether the safety latch malfunctioned that day. However the circumstance, he had his finger on the trigger, with the barrel pointed directly at Mel's head when he handed the nail gun up to Mel. The nail gun discharged striking Mel in the head and lodging nails deep inside his brain.

Lula was notified of the accident by a Worumbo mill supervisor. She was told Mel had been rushed to the hospital in Lewiston. That night she and her children stood around Mel's hospital bed praying he would survive. When the doctor came to speak with the family that evening he told them to pray that God took him. His brain had been severely damaged and would never function. Mel was brain dead.

God took Mel the next day. Lula and her family were in shock. They were shattered. She had lost her one true love, her rock her gentle giant. A soft spoken man with the warmest of hearts who loved everyone. He believed deeply in his religious faith. Mel had never swore or said anything harmful to or about anyone in his 56 years. Family, faith and work was

Mel's entire life. He had a dry sense of humor which his friends and family totally enjoyed. One day Lula was complaining about using her wringer washing machine. She told Mel it was a wish of hers to someday have an automatic washer and dryer. The laundry task took a complete day to accomplish with washing each load in the wringer washer and then hanging them upon the clothesline to dry.

The very next day when Mel came home from work he found Lula folding clothes in the bedroom. Mel told Lula that he had bought her that washer and dryer she had wanted. Lula was more than excited. She kept asking Mel where they were? Mel told her they were sitting on the kitchen table. What ? Lula immediately ran into the kitchen. There she discovered a pair of washer and dryer salt and pepper shakers, proudly displayed on the kitchen table. After a few disappointed minutes Lula and Mel were laughing together over his practical joke.

Mel knew Lula collected S & P shakers so with his dry sense of humor, Mel thought he was providing both her wishes. Lula had collected over 50 sets of Salt and Pepper shakers since their wedding. Mel even built Lula a lighted display case for her collection on their living room wall. That was her Mel.

Whatever Lula wanted, he tried his best to accommodate. The distance from the mill to their house was one mile. Many days Mel would walk to work leaving Lula the car in case of an emergency. Perhaps Mel's only flaw was his poor memory. He often forgot things. Lula would ask him to pick up 3 items at the store and Mel would usually come home with two of the items she had asked for. Lula's Irish temper would flare up resting on Mel's shoulders. He let her cool down from the disappointment then calmly return to the store for the missing item. This he always did without complaint. If the children misbehaved and needed punishment, Lula and Mel disciplined very differently. I remember my Aunt Idolyne, Uncle Stanley and my mother distinctly telling me how they preferred being struck by the belt or branch switch, Lula's method, than having a talk with their father. Mel did not yell or criticize them. Instead of a physical scolding he shared with them how disappointed he was in their behavior.

Mel disliked anyone telling a lie whether it be white or not, he believed telling the truth was always best.

Mama used to say that after a belt whipping by Nana she refused to cry. Disappointing her father would result in a flood of tears. Mel's tombstone was engraved with the words " All Who Knew Him Loved Him." I regret not being able to remember my grandfather. The day he was hurt Mel had come home to have lunch with Lula and Deborah.

Apparently my cousin Pamela, 3 months younger than I and myself were at my grandparents' house that day. After finishing his lunch Nana said Mel delighted in playing with his grandchildren.

Pamela was 16 months old and I was 19 months old. Just the right ages to be tossed up in the air and caught by this gentle giant. At 6'4 and over 300 pounds our grandfather must have seemed huge to us. He joked with my mother that Pamela and I confused him as who was who. Mel thought we looked more like twins than cousins. That day would be the last time Mama, Nana Pamela, Deborah and I saw him full of life.

CHAPTER NINE

ANOTHER WIDOW

LULA became a widow at 56, living in an unfinished house, bringing up her four year old granddaughter. Stanley turned over the house to his mother and daughter. He helped Lula work on completing the construction. Lula had no income in which to raise Deborah. She was too young to receive social security. Mel and Lula had not legally adopted their granddaughter therefore Deborah was not entitled to any benefits. Lula went to court to adopted Deborah and become her legal guardian.

Stanley had a new family to support. He signed away his parental rights for his mother to raise his daughter. Francis was persuaded to do the same for the sake of her child. Once Deborah was legally adopted, Lula was able to get social security benefits for her. Lula also turned her hobby of braiding rugs into a small business. She would purchase barrels of woolen scraps from the Worumbo woolen mill for her rugs.

The sizes of the braided rugs varied from 3' x 5 ' up to 18 ' x 20 '. Lula also would custom size a rug upon a buyer's request. I believe the highest price she ever charged was $50.00 for the 18'x20' size braided rug. Every year for her church's annual country fair, Lula donated one of her large braided rugs for their fundraising raffle. To be eligible to win the braided rug you had to purchase 5 woolen pot holders for $1.00. This purchase qualified you for five chances to win the rug. The handmade pot holders were also made and donated by my Nana.

One year a church member bought 10 chances in his dog's name. Oh yes, his dog won the beautiful 18'x20' braided rug, disappointing many women in the church. The story of his dog's win was retold often in the church.

Lula had become diabetic in her late forties. Every morning, she injected herself with insulin to keep it under control. Knowing she would be away from her refrigerated insulin for a long period of time, Lula always carried candy bars or hard candy in her purse to prevent going into diabetic shock. Keeping on a strict diabetic diet was a real struggle for Lula. My Nana loved to bake desserts for her family. She enjoyed eating her own baked goods even though sweets were off limits. Homemade doughnuts, pies, cakes and cookies were forever prevalent in Nana's kitchen. Lula learned to cook with lard, eggs and lots of sugar. Lula's 5 foot frame had a battle against her weight her entire life.

We never really knew how much Nana weighed. I would guess it fluctuated between 190 and 225. Lula's exercise consisted of walking the 50 feet to her garden or clothesline. Her rug braiding kept Lula seated for hours. There was always a large bag of Wether's caramel candies next to her chair, for a quick snack. How she loved those caramel candies. In the evenings I remember seeing Nana massage her legs and feet with rubbing alcohol.

She told me the leg pain was from poor circulation due to the diabetes. Lula was in her sixties and visiting our second floor apartment when she stumbled and fell down a flight of stairs breaking her right arm. As her right hand was predominant this caused problems. My mother Mildred offered to help out for the eight weeks her arm was in a cast. She did not mind the cooking, laundry or cleaning. One task Mildred hated was giving Lula the daily insulin injections. Mildred had never been fond of needles to begin with, Lula had her practice injections on an orange until she felt comfortable.

Nana was a tough woman having survived many operations and a risky childbirth.

Lula assured Mildred she would do fine. Mama took the syringe, carefully filled it with insulin. She found a safe section on Nana's stomach, jabbed the needle in and slowly released the medicine. Lula never flinched, Mildred was covered in sweat. She thanked Mildred reminding her to come back the same time each day to do the procedure again.

Mildred was relieved when the cast was removed. Without a cast, Lula could regain her injection routine. Ironically, Mildred had to reestablish her duties only 6 months later when Lula fell in her own home and broke her left arm. This time Lula was able to vaccinate herself only needing two steady hands to fill the syringe with insulin. The filling of the syringe Mildred could do easily.

Deborah had a lovely soprano voice. She took singing and piano lessons with a friend of Lula's who happened to be a music teacher.

Mel had always been involved with music. He sang in a choral group, played guitar and harmonica. Lula played the organ and Mildred played piano. Deborah enjoyed singing and playing piano at music recitals for over five years. I loved attending those recitals. The best musical memories were the Sunday singalongs at Nana's house. Every Sunday after attending church we ate Sunday dinner then Deborah, Nana, Mama and I would gather around Nana's old player piano and sing gospel songs. The self-player function didn't work therefore all the piano playing was done by Mama. We usually sang our favorite church hymns with a finale of popular Broadway songs.

Singing around the piano was a great family bonding time that I will never forget. One of Nana's good church friends was Ethelyn Flaws. She played the organ at our church. Ethelyn was also my 4th and 5th grade school teacher. Durham Elementary School in the 1960's had a small pupil enrollment. Many of the grades were combined into one classroom. One teacher would be responsible for teaching multiple grades at a time.

Another noteworthy fact about Ethelyn, she had a nephew who was gaining recognition as an author. His name Stephen King. King had attended Lisbon High School with Lula's nephew. When Lula heard about Ethelyn's nephew publishing the book " Carrie" about a school girl she wanted to read it. Naïve Lula had the impression that it would be something like a Rebecca of Sunny Brook Farm type story, gentle, kind and clean cut. Not ! By the time she had read the first chapter Lula was horrified. How could Ethelyn's nephew write about a girl's menstrual cycle ? she said. Lula refused to finish the book. She told Deborah and I not to read it. This of course intrigued us. It wasn't long before Deb and I would take turns sneaking the book away to read it. We liked it.

By the time I attended Lisbon High School in the 70's, Stephen King was extremely popular and the book " Carrie" was going to be made into a major movie. Deb and I were more like sisters than cousins. Mama and I lived next door in the house Stanley had converted from a garage. We did not have a telephone in our house but Nana had one. One problem, it was a party line. A party line phone circuit is shared by more than one subscriber. This means absolutely NO PRIVACY. Each subscriber had their own individual ring. Two rings meant it was Nana's call.

One, three, four or five rings were calls for others on the line. A major problem was that people who shared a party line circuit could pick up the receiver and listen to everyone's conversations. Worse thing was if someone was talking on the phone line the other subscribers could not make a phone call until they hung up. If an emergency occurred your party line knew before anyone else. At certain times up to four lines were open for everyone to listen in on conversations without permissions. Deb and I found it amusing to listen in on people's conversations until Nana caught us.

During winter snowstorms if our electricity was out for long periods of time, Deb and I used the walkie talkies,we had received at Christmas, to keep in touch. I was 16 years old when our own telephone was installed. Mama became concerned about Nana's health especially her diabetic condition. She wanted her 70 year old mother to be able to reach her in case of an emergency or illness. Mama requested a single circuit line. It cost more money each month but assured total privacy.

Since it was primarily for emergencies, Deb and I were restricted to limited time periods for our conversations. Lula continued driving well into her seventies. Her trips consisted of church, the doctor's office and the grocery store. We would laugh on the occasions when she would complain about all the old people driving on the road. Fact was the people Nana spoke about were usually years younger than her.

Lula had known her neighbors John and Lena Patrick for over 30 years. A brother and sister who lived nearby in a dilapidated old farmhouse. Lena was born with strabismus or crossed eyes. She was a sweet and kind lady.

Despite Lena's poor vision she cleaned, washed clothes and cooked all their meals. On Halloween, Nana and Mama took Deb and I trick or treating at their house. We were told to politely accept whatever Lena gave us, then discard the food at home. Nana was afraid with her impaired eyesight Lena may not have put in the correct ingredients when baking. John had cows for milk and a large vegetable garden. In the 1936 flood when the bridge between the two towns of Lisbon Falls and Durham washed away, John transported people across the river in his small 6 person boat. Bridge repairs took several months to complete. Durham residents working at the Worumbo woolen mill like my grandfather Mel used John Patrick's boat service daily. After Mel and Lena had both passed away, Lula offered to help John Patrick. He was in his late eighties. Lula drove him to his doctor's appointments and the grocery store. Once or twice a week she prepared meals for him and did some cleaning.

When John Patrick died, he willed the farmhouse plus a few acres of land to Lula. She sold the farmhouse but held onto the land as an investment. Having the option to sell the land to pay for any unforeseen health needs eased her mind.

CHAPTER TEN

Together Again

EARLY Spring 1979, Lula's health began to fail. Her diabetes began affecting Lula's legs and feet dramatically. Her children insisted Lula stop driving. On Mildred's days off she took Lula to appointments or shopping. It became quite a struggle for Lula to walk even a short distance. One day, Mildred noticed a drastic change in skin color on Lula's left leg. The leg was grayish in color and cold to the touch. She persuaded Lula to see a doctor immediately. The doctor came to the conclusion her leg had no circulation and must be amputated.

Lula had suspected this to be true, She had refused to accept in her mind what her body was telling her. Lula's leg was amputated. While Lula was in the hospital Mildred purchased a walker for her to use at home. Stanley built her a ramp to the kitchen door. Idolyne brought food and Deborah helped rearrange Lula's house to accommodate the walker and perhaps a wheelchair later on.

Once Lula came home the situation grew worse. Mildred and the other family members tried to visit every day to make sure she was recuperating properly. The doctor advised frequent walker use to help her circulation. He feared blood clots could form. Lula was constantly worried about her living arrangements and feared having to leave her home. Lula was stubborn. She refused to have anyone live with her.

At 79 years old her greatest concern was being sent to a nursing home facility. Mildred reassured her, she would not let that happen. Lula decided to sell the land she inherited from John Patrick to help cover medical costs.

When my husband and I built our house next door, we had no mortgage. We had used all or our combined savings for the construction. To help Nana financially, we took out a loan to purchase the land she wanted to sell. We viewed it as an investment for the future of our children. Losing her leg took its toll on Lula both physically and mentally. She became quite depressed.

She had always been the strong one, the matriarch. Lula loved being a Nana. Her grandchildren and greatgrandchildren brought great joys into her life. It was Nana we went to for comfort if our parents didn't understand. Nana was the one who pulled out those loos baby teeth for the grandkids.

Nana calmly distracted us by talking about her childhood as her chubby tissue covered fingers gripped tightly onto our dangly tooth. One swift tug, the tooth was out before we even knew it. Lula enjoyed baking with the youngest members of her family whether the finished creation was a success or not. We still ate it.

For me it was the peanut butter cookies we made together each month. Now every time I make them, I think of my Nana. The temper and disciplinary actions Lula had shown as a parent were nonexistent as a grandmother. Nana thought we grandkids could do no wrong.

On a beautiful Sunday afternoon in May 1979, what the doctor had feared might occur, did happen. A blood clot traveled from her amputated leg up to Nana's heart. We came back from a family outing to find an ambulance, lights flashing, parked outside Nana's kitchen door.

Panicked, I immediately ran down the path from our house to hers. She was in cardiac arrest and being transported to the hospital.

Mama called her siblings, to tell them about Nana's condition. She then followed the ambulance to the hospital. Within minutes of Lula's arrival her children were by her side. For the next 7 days family members took turns staying by Nana's bedside. Deb and I had small children, who were not allowed in the hospital. Our husbands watched the children a couple hours each night so that we may visit with her. Doctors decided to implant a pacemaker into Nana's chest to regulate her heart.

After the procedure, Stanley and his sisters were at Lula's bedside when she seemed to briefly "pass over" into unconsciousness. Lula looked up at her son and clearly stated, "Melbourne I see the gate. " The statement upset Stanley tremendously. Hearing those words made him leave the hospital room and go sit in his truck in the hospital parking lot. He felt like she had gone on already to heaven with his father. The next day was June 6th, Mildred's 58th birthday.

Mildred arrived early at the hospital. She was prepared to stay until the evening. Lula was still sleeping when Mildred entered the hospital room. A nurse came in to wake Lula. She needed to give her some medication. Lula awoke. She looked around and saw Mildred sitting at her bedside. " Happy Birthday, not a very good way to spend your birthday. " whispered Lula, her voice cracking. Mildred just smiled back replying it was okay to spend her birthday there. Her mother was noticeably drowsy and fatigued.

Lula's facial color was a grayish tone. Mildred sensed her mother was fading away. Suddenly she heard Lula murmur, "no peace, I need peace. " An hour later Lula joined her beloved Melbourne in heaven. We had expected Nana's passing but it still was upsetting. She was the only grandparent I had ever known. Mama and I had lived a few yards away from Nana for 20 years.

Nana had been the matriarch of our entire family. Her role would never be replaced. Since my grandfather's death, Lula was the sole parent to her children. The loss was shattering to all the family members. Our only comfort was we believed she was finally at peace, no more pain. She was walking hand in hand with her dear Mel once again.

CHAPTER ELEVEN

MILDRED CRAIG HENDERSON

MILDRED Louise Craig was born on June 6th 1921. The first child of Lula and Melbourne Craig. She was born about 9 months from their wedding on September 18, 1920. Lula and Mel were delighted with their newborn baby girl. The baby was given the first name of Lula's mother Mildred Mcintosh and her middle name was after Louise Small, Lula's aunt.

Family members agreed that her looks favored Mel. Since Lula had helped raise her younger siblings she felt quite comfortable around the newborn. Mildred weighed 6 pounds. She fit comfortably into the baby gowns that Lula had sewn. Mildred was also the first grandchild on the Mcintosh side. Subsequently, Lula's mother became known, from then on, as Gram Mac. Lila and Silas Craig were her grandparents on Mel's side. Lila became known as Grammy Craig. Lula and Mel were living in a small two-story house below the hill where Lula's dear friend Mrs. Beals and her son Olin lived.

On warm summer days, Lula proudly pushed Mildred's carriage up the long steep road leading to Mrs. Beals, to show her daughter to Mrs. Beals. Mrs. Beals truly enjoyed their visits. She loved being able to rock a baby in her arms again. Son Olin had never married.

Aside from the earlier mentions episode, where Lula's baby girl recovered from a seizure Mildred was a healthy happy baby.

Mel took pleasure in carpentry as well as mechanics. When Lula was pregnant, he built a beautiful cradle for the new baby. On Mildred's 1st birthday, Mel gifted his daughter with a child's rocking chair he had made. Many decades later, the rocking chair is a cherished piece of furniture in my own home.

Lula sang lullabies to Mildred, although it was Mel's deep baritone voice she drifted off to sleep by. As the years passed it became apparent that Mildred was a true daddy's girl. She totally idolized her father. Mildred followed him everywhere. She often sat quietly on his lap as he read or sang to her. It was understood in the 1920's, girls wore dresses and were expected to maintain interests in cooking, sewing or being a mother's little helper. Mildred would prefer to sneak out into her father's garage to watch him work on one of his automobiles. She found comfort in Mel's tranquil manner.

A pleasant contrast to Lula's quick temper and sometimes critical judgements. She ruled the house with a stern hand. Mel intervened when he saw Lula getting frustrated with the children. Mildred recalled one time she had forgotten a bible verse she was to recite in a Sunday School play. Lula was quite upset while Mel applauded Mildred for trying and doing the best she could. At age four, Mildred was thrilled to welcome a new member to the family. Her baby sister Idolyne was born. The new baby had darker hair and a button nose much like her mother Lula. Mel did not seem to mind that he was surrounded by females.

By the time son M. Stanley came along, the girls were old enough to help Lula with his many needs. Idolyne was 5 years old and Mildred was nearly ten. Mildred became best friends with her neighbor and schoolmate Mary E. The neighbors were immigrants who recently had arrived from Czechoslovakia to work in the woolen mill.

Lisbon and Durham became home to a large Slovak community. As schoolmates Mildred and Mary would walk to the one room schoolhouse next door to their homes.

Mary and Mildred lived a short walk from one another. This meant they frequently visited each other's houses. Mary loved going to the Craig household because Lula was always baking sugary treats for them to eat. Lula enjoyed the continuous giggles and silly girl games they would play together. Mildred found Mary E.'s home to be less appealing. she said Mary's father looked angry all the time. He never smiled and she felt he was extremely harsh with his children. Mrs. E. observed traditional Slovak cooking methods. One day Mildred smelled something familiar cooking on Mrs. E.'s stove. Mary informed her it was chicken noodle soup. Mildred like chicken noodle soup, especially how Lula made it. She was willing to give Mrs. E.'s soup recipe a taste. Her appetite when Mrs. E. lifted the cover of the boiling soup pot.

All Mildred could see were chicken feet and a chicken head bopping around inside the soup pot. Mildred politely refused the soup, saying she was not hungry. As best friends do, Mary and Mildred shared secrets. Mildred confessed to smoking a cigarette she had been given by another classmate. Mary's secret was darker and more painful. Her father demanded Mary and her brother work many chores without complaining. Mary had a small petite build. She did not have the strength her brother did. Mary told Mildred if they disobeyed their father, he would beat them. Mildred was used to being hit with a belt or Lula's yardstick. she didn't consider that a beating.

Mary took off her blouse to show Mildred her misshaped back. Her back revealed an obvious bulge on Mary's shoulder. She told Mildred her father had tied her to a post in the barn and beat her. The result was Mary's broken collarbone. Mildred was stunned.

After hearing about the beatings, Mildred decided not to let Mary leave the Craig household when she visited. When the time came for Mary to go home, Mildred hid Mary. Lula knew Mary's parents would be upset. She insisted Mildred tell her where Mary was. Mildred refused. She offered to have a belt whipping instead of making known Mary's hiding place. Mary heard her friend's plea. She didn't want Mildred punished because of her. She voluntarily came out of hiding. Mildred then locked the door and stood in front of it. She begged Lula to not let Mary leave. Of course, Lula just thought the girls wanted more playtime together. Then Mildred told her mother Mary's secret. Lula told the girls she would walk both of them up to Mary's house. She'd explain to Mary's parents that it wasn't Mary's fault that she was late.

When they arrived at the E. house, Lula and Mrs. E. carried on a friendly conversation. Mildred never knew if Mary received any punishment for being late. Mary did not mention her home life to Mildred ever again.

Many years later, Mama and I saw an old gentleman wearing a fedora hat walking from Lisbon Falls towards Durham. She stopped and gave him a ride to his home which was a short distance from our house. The man was Mary's father. He never smiled or talked much during the entire car ride. He did say " thank you" as he exited our car.

Mary E. wed and moved to New Hampshire. She and Mildred stayed in touch by letters or phone for the next thirty years. Mary could never have children. Mildred often wondered if the physical abuse, Mary had received as a child, was a factor.

Many Slovak students attended Mildred's high school. Her senior year, she began dating a young Slovak boy named Andy V. Lula and Mel really liked him. Andy was respectful, polite and rather shy. He and Mildred's dates consisted of sitting on the living room sofa listening to the radio and eating Lula's treats. Little brother Stanley, idolized Andy.

Andy took the time to talk and play games with him. Stanley loved it when Any's change fell out of his pants pocket into the sofa cushions. He waited patiently for Andy to leave the house before ravaging the sofa cushions to collect the money. Sometimes, Mildred felt Andy purposely tossed change out as not to disappoint Stanley. Andy's parents were very friendly and courteous towards Mildred. As their dating progressed, it became evident both sets of parents were in total agreement on one particular matter. They believed Mildred and Andy should never be allowed to marry.

A perspective lost on two young people, who were falling deeply in love. In defiance, when Mildred turned 21, Andy proposed. They actually became engaged. The disparity was not cultural. The objections by the parents were strictly their religious differences. Andy was Catholic. Mildred was Protestant. Andy's parents insisted he must marry a Catholic girl. Lula and Mel were both Protestants who attended different churches. Lula attended a Congregationalist church and Mel attended the Methodist church. He had stepped away from the Shiloh church his parents attended finding the Methodist principles suited him better. Lula and Mel's faith and religious beliefs meant a great deal to them.

Andy's parents were steadfast Catholics. The turmoil began to take a toll on the young couple. Andy suggested to Mildred she might have to convert to Catholicism for them to marry. Mildred asked her father's opinion on Andy's request. Mel expressed the religious factor was too deep a divide.

Mel conveyed to Mildred if she were to convert to marry in the Catholic church, he would not give his blessing. Her father said he would not attend the wedding. This declaration devastated Mildred. She could not envision her wedding ceremony without her beloved Dad. Andy was experiencing a similar standoff. His parents emphatically expressed that they would not condone or give their blessing if he married a non-Catholic girl. Mildred was a fine girl to date but not a girl to marry.

The friction started to tear away at the love struck couple. Mildred expressed doubts about a marriage surviving their families extensive discord. Andy became deeply depressed. The young couple torn apart by their parents demands decided to break up. WWII was raging overseas. Andy to join the army. Andy spoke to Mildred before he left. Andy told her that he didn't care if he is killed in the war, he did not want to live without Mildred.

Mildred had attended a hairdressing school and received her beautician's license. Before the war came, she interned at a local salon. During the war years people would leave their primary jobs and began working at trades to support the war effort. Mildred worked at the Worumbo woolen mill. The woolen cloth was used to make pea coats for the US Navy. I recall Mama telling about that period in her life when she'd come home with hands and arms stained blue. The indigo blue dye was used to color the US Navy uniforms. Apparently, it took weeks for the indigo blue dye to wash or wear off.

Meanwhile, Andy's parents had given his army mailing address to a young Catholic girl from their church who had a crush on him. Before long their correspondence turned into affection. When Andy came home from the war, the girl was anxiously waiting for him.

Andy's parents aggressively encouraged the relationship. He soon proposed to the girl. They married a few months after he had returned home. A salon customer who had known them both told Mildred about Andy's marriage. Her sadness was short-lived. Mildred knew Andy was a nice descent guy who deserved a chance to be happy. Mildred had started dating six months after the breakup. Her relationship with her father remained strong, even though her personal independence grew. Mildred vowed never to let a relationship influence her objectivity again. One young man she dated tried to impress her with his fast driving. She insisted he slow down and stop " showing off ". He kept right on speeding. Mildred reached over turned off the ignition key and blew the car engine. He was furious. She reminded him, he had been warned to slow down. They never dated again.

Another young man named Bill, really liked Mildred. She found him to be too possessive. He lived with his widowed mother, who doted on his every need. Mildred and Bill enjoyed going out to dinner and dancing at nightclubs. He became extremely jealous, if Mildred talked to other people, male or female. Their last date together was at a local nightclub where many of Mildred's friends frequented.

While sipping on her rum and coke, Mildred discreetly began looking around the room for a familiar face. Bill became irate. He asked if she was looking to find someone better than him. She was tired of his mistrustful behavior. Mildred remarked, " perhaps I am". Bill stood up announcing they were leaving. Mildred told him to go right ahead she intended to stay and finish her rum and coke. Bill left her at the nightclub.

Undaunted by Bill's departure, Mildred ordered a second drink. She stayed another two hours before calling a taxi to take her home. Bill was history. A couple other fellows tried to win her heart but she was not interested. Mildred focused on her career. She opened Mildred's Beauty Shop in her second floor apartment. The apartment was directly above Uncle Bob and Ethel's first floor apartment. Bob had maintained his heavy drinking. Ethel managed to tolerate his drinking. When he became loud or obnoxious, Ethel knew Mildred was right upstairs. Many times Ethel came knocking at Mildred's door. She would ask to stay there until Bob sobered up again. Mildred liked Ethel. She felt sorry about the abusive childhood Ethel had endured. As a teenager I asked Mama why Ethel seemed afraid and fearful. That's when Mama explained how Ethel's father had beaten her and forced her to sleep with him.

The times Ethel went to Mildred's apartment for safety increased. She would sit and talk with Mildred for 2-3 hours until she heard Bob's loud snoring from downstairs. That is when she felt safe to return. Ethel would carefully walked back down to their apartment to find Bob passed out on the toilet or bathroom floor. She routinely took a blanket and covered Bob before going to sleep. In the morning Mildred often heard them laughing and giggling like newlyweds. She missed those happy sounds after their divorce. Even with Ethel several blocks away, she and Mildred remained friends.

CHAPTER TWELVE

TUP

IN 1950 Mildred and some girlfriends were at a dance club in Bath, Maine. One girlfriend worked at Bath Iron Works. She knew several of the club's patrons. Mildred loved to dance. She never refused an offer to hit the dance floor. That night Mildred sipped her drink, tapped her feet to the music hoping to participate. The next time her friend walked back from the bar, she brought back more than drinks. She had with her a BIW co-worker named Thornton G. Henderson. Mr. Henderson said he preferred being called Tup.

Mildred had an immediate attraction to Tup. Even with a thriving business, the 30 year old Mildred, hoped to settle down and start a family someday. Tup asked Mildred to dance. They danced together all evening long. Tup was a charmer with a good sense of humor. A Bath native he had spent four years in the Army, fighting the war in Japan. Upon his discharge he returned to work with his brother at the Kennebec Greenhouse in his hometown of Bath.

Tup was living in his family home two blocks from the greenhouse. After his mother died, Tup's father remarried and moved into the new wife's house. Mildred and Tup began spending all their free time together. A favorite date night was dinner and dancing at clubs or grange halls. Just a few weeks into their dating, Mildred and Tup won a dance contest at the local grange hall doing their favorite dance step The Lindy Hop. Thanksgiving was approaching which meant the prize to salute their victory was a turkey.

Mildred was thrilled to win until she discovered it was a live turkey.

Tup and Mildred immediately took the live bird over to her mother's house. Lula had no qualms about slaughtering the turkey for Thanksgiving. Growing up, I heard this dance winning story every year at Thanksgiving time.

For unexplained reasons, in the spring of '51, Tup and Mildred drifted apart. Tup began spending more time with his male friends and Mildred's increasing clientele at the beauty shop kept her very busy. Many of her regular customers were Worumbo mill workers, she had worked alongside during the war years. Mildred's rise in customers forced the need to hire an assistant. Idolyne now divorced with a child had been temporarily laid off from the Lewiston shoe factory. Mildred decided to hire Idolyne to clean the shop between customers.

In those days there were no hair rollers or quick perms. Bobby pins or hair pins made all the waves and curls. The hair perms were very time consuming, involving each strand of hair being placed between rubber pads wrapped in tin foil and dosed with a smelly liquid. One of Idolyne's jobs included disinfecting the brushes, combs and discarding the perm foil. She also needed to sweep and dispose of hair cuttings from the shop floor.

Idolyne expressed her dislike for these tasks. She was overjoyed two months later when the shoe factory rehired her. Mildred was very fond of her customers. Women came not only for hair care solutions but sometimes therapy and support. Customers spilling the beans about their love lives or family problems was a normal occurrence. Mildred accepted the gossip as part of the business. She tried to answer their questions or offer suggestions to them.

Two clients in particular, she could never forget. Their stories were told many times to me over the years. The first incident concerned a woman who found out at age 51 that she was pregnant. In the 1950's a pregnancy at 51 was considered extremely dangerous to both mother and baby. The woman already had two sons ages 21 and 23 years old. During a comb out one day, this woman burst into tears. She told Mildred her tragic situation. In the woman's mind this pregnancy was a death sentence. She had made out her will, said her goodbyes to family and had even laid out burial clothes for her funeral. When her husband came that day to pick her up from Mildred's Beauty Shop he was melancholy and looked like he had not slept in months. As the time grew closer to the birth, Mildred heard about the woman's funeral plans. The plans included the child because the woman believed it could not survive.

Mama was happy to tell me the conclusion of this morbid recollection was that the woman gave birth to a healthy baby boy and his mother lived to see him grow into adulthood. After he was born the woman came into the shop to show Mildred her baby. She was embarrassed to concede how foolish her plans had been. The second encounter Mama loved to tell me was about a customer who was having an affair with the husband of another client. Mildred had to be particularly careful when making appointments for the two ladies. Mildred tried not to book them on the same day but unfortunately an incident occurred when the wife was leaving the shop just as the mistress came in. This exchange clearly revealed that the wife did not suspect anything because the mistress was a close childhood friend of the wife's.

The majority of regular beauty shop customers were less dramatic. They had known Mildred for several years. One of these regulars actually informed Mildred about Tup's first marriage. She was a friend of Tup's new wife. Mildred had not seen Tup or heard from him for several weeks. Nonetheless, this unanticipated news bothered her. In the fall of 1952, Mildred received a phone call from Tup. The conversation began with small talk about work and friends. Suddenly, Tup asked if Mildred would like to go out for dinner and dancing sometime. Mildred immediately responded with," I don't date married men !

Awkward silence on the other end of the phone. Tup apologized for not telling her about his marriage. He insisted they were in the process of getting a divorce. Mildred told him when the divorce papers were legally signed and published in the newspaper, she may consider a date. She abruptly hung up the phone. A month later, Mildred read his divorce decree published in a local newspaper.

Two days later, Tup called her again. He asked if she had seen the printed divorce notice. She answered yes. Mildred agreed to date him. Quickly, Mildred and Tup became serious. He told her the first marriage had been a drunken mistake. Tup told Mildred he had never stopped caring about her. Mildred knew Tup was a charmer and jokester but he did seem sincere about having a relationship. He began spending nights at her apartment. She would meet Tup at the greenhouse for sex among the flowers.

Mama conveyed to me on several occasions, I was most likely conceived in the greenhouse among the Christmas poinsettias. Mildred had always wanted to have children. As a teen one of her ovaries had been removed and the remaining one packed in penicillin, leading her to believe she could never conceive. Therefore, Mildred and Tup never practiced any birth control methods. Early February 1954 Mildred went to see a doctor. Her menstrual periods had stopped coming. The pregnancy test came back positive. At 33 years old Mildred was going to have a baby. All her friends and relatives had married right out of high school or soon after, they had teenagers now. Idolyne had a nine year old. Stanley had a third baby on the way and planning to wed in April. Tup was surprised and excited.

Lula was very critical and insisted they marry soon. Mel was a bit disappointed but looked forward to another grandchild. Mildred felt perhaps her parents were holding her to a different standard because she was the oldest. Her siblings had gone through similar circumstances when they wed. They married on April 3,1954. Certainly not the wedding Mildred had dreamed about in her youth.

The two of them quietly went to the justice of the peace. Tup wore a three piece suit and Mildred wore a simple tan suit with a white carnation pinned on the collar. The ceremony took less than ten minutes. Mildred moved into Tup's family home in Bath. They shared the house with Tup's old Boxer dog, Darcy. Mildred and Darcy had issues with one another. Darcy was very jealous of Mildred. On many occasions when the dog had joined them, Tup would put Darcy in the back seat letting Mildred snuggle up close to Tup as he was driving.

Within minutes a foul odor reeked from the backseat drifting steadily into the front. The stench was unbearable.

Each time it happened, Mildred quickly slid over to the passenger side to open a window. Like clockwork, Darcy would immediately jump into the front seat shoving Mildred aside to be able to sit next to Tup. Tup found great humor in this routine. Mildred failed to find any of it funny. After too many of those dates she insisted they leave the dog at home. She really was not looking forward to sharing her husband and new baby with this obsessive dog. As the baby's arrival date grew closer, Mildred became quite anxious about how Darcy may act around the newborn. Would he be jealous enough to bite her or worse ? Each morning when Tup left for the greenhouse he was prompted to take the dog along. There was a barn beside the greenhouse where his brother kept a horse named Randy. Randy and Darcy got along just fine. The dog would stay in the barn while Tup and is brother Melvin worked in the greenhouse.

Unfortunately, smoking was not considered a danger to pregnant women in 1954. Mildred preferred to smoke more and eat less. She never had to wear traditional maternity clothes due to the fact she only gained 14 pounds. In fact, the day before I was born my mother stopped at the local market to purchase a few items. Mama wore a black sweater and black skirt that tied around the waist. The store keeper chatted with her for several minutes during the visit. A couple days later my father went into the same market to handout cigars to celebrate my birth. The store keeper was totally surprised, he had no idea Mildred was pregnant.

Back in the1950's, a woman went to the doctor to verify a pregnancy. She usually did not go back to see the doctor until labor started. On a hot and very humid August day in 1954, Mildred started to feel uncomfortable. She began having pains in her abdomen ranging in various degrees of discomfort. First a twinge that became like a severe cramping ache. Mildred called her mother Lula for advice. Lula told Mildred to have Tup bring her to the hospital as soon as possible. Lula arrived at the hospital right after Mildred was admitted.

While waiting for the doctor to arrive, Mildred told Lula she felt a wetness. She suspected her water broke. Lula lifted the bedsheet and looked below Mildred's stomach expecting to find a clear wet spot. Lula was alarmed to see a large bloody mass instead. Having many mid-wife experiences plus birthing four children of her own, Lula knew this was not normal. Something was very wrong. Lula called the nurse over showing her Mildred's continuous blood leakage. Mildred started to feel panicked about what they were seeing.

When the nurse went to find the doctor, Lula told Mildred she believed the afterbirth was coming. They needed to get the baby out quickly. Lula was remembering her stillbirth. She did not want Mildred to go through that heartbreak. Once the doctor arrived, Tup and Lula were sent out to the waiting room. Mildred was rushed into the delivery room.

Dr. Twaddle was an old school doctor in his seventies. He instructed the nurses to cover Mildred from head to toe with sterile gowns and foot covers for the delivery. Dr. Twaddle placed her feet into the metal stirrups. He told the anesthesiologist to prepare the nitrous oxide or laughing gas to ease the labor pains.

A rubber mask distributing nitrous oxide was placed over Mildred's face. She was told to breathe deeply when a contraction was felt. This method released gas into her system to dull the pain. Mildred inhaled a whiff of gas with each pain. Scared and sensing urgency in the situation, Mildred uttered a silent prayer. Finally, several pushes later, the baby was delivered. Since Mildred had only gained 14 pounds no stitches were needed. The baby was hastily cleaned, tossed into a hospital bassinet and whisked away to the nursery.

Dr. Twaddle pushed down repeatedly on Mildred's abdomen. He needed to make sure the fetal membranes and placenta was expelled from her uterus. Mildred did not complain. She'd heard some horrific birthing stories. Women had collapsed and died from toxins building up from partial placentas left inside the womb. She knew Dr. Twaddle was being thorough and cautious by making sure all the afterbirth had been expelled.

He was about to leave, when Mildred asked him a couple questions, " Is it a boy or girl ? How much does it weight ?" The gruff old physician shot back, " girl, she'll probably go about 2 or 3 pounds !" Mildred was delighted with the news of a girl but weighing only 2 or 3 pounds frightened her. Truth was, I weighed in at 4 pounds 6 ounces and 18 inches long. It never was determined if the low birth rate was due to my mother's heavy smoking or was I premature ?

Mildred was taken back to her hospital room and told to rest. Tup and Lula watched through the nursery's glass window at the baby girl in the bassinet.

In the days that followed, friends and relatives stopped by the hospital nursery to see the new baby. Idolyne viewed the tiny girl before visiting with Mildred in her hospital room. Idolyne was always brutally honest, never sugarcoating her remarks. When Mildred asked what the baby looked like, Idolyne replied, " she has a real big head, tiny body with arms and legs that look like uncooked frankfurters. Whew ! With a description like that, Mildred was even more concerned about her baby. Of course others told Mildred the baby was cute and tiny. Yes everyone had seen her baby but Mildred.

Dr. Twaddle insisted his patients stay in bed for a week to ten days after giving birth. He let them dangle their feet over the side of the bed after two days. Mildred felt fine just a little tired. Her mental state of mind was very different. She became deeply depressed. Her baby was in an incubator unable to leave the nursery. Mildred was prohibited from leaving her hospital room. On the seventh night a young candy striper found Mildred crying. She inquired what the problem was. Mildred told her, she had not even seen her baby yet.

The volunteer quickly left the room, returning 5 minutes later with the baby in her arms. She made Mildred promise never to tell anyone what she had done. Mildred promised not to tell. While holding the newborn in her arms, the candy striper pulled back the receiving blanket to show Mildred her daughter. Although a quick peek, Mildred was happy to finally see her baby girl.

Tup and Mildred had not discussed any names for the baby. Mildred had liked the old bible name Rhoda.

She told the staff worker who asked the name for hospital records, Rhoda Lee would be the baby's name. Tup came later that day asking what name she had chosen. Mildred told him the name was Rhoda Lee. Tup suggested his mother's name Bertha be given as a middle name. Mildred explained, Rhoda was the first and Lee was the middle name. Then she told a white lie to Tup saying it was too late to change the hospital paperwork for the birth certificate. Mildred thought Bertha was too old a name for a baby.

Mildred told him maybe the next child but Tup said after seeing what she had gone through, one child would be fine with him. The birth was ten days ago and Mildred had still not officially seen the baby. Tup was furious. He called Dr. Twaddle to complain. Within minutes a nurse came with a wheelchair for Mildred's ride to the nursery to see her baby. Tup happily wheeled her to the nursery viewing window. She was not allowed to hold the baby but the nurses told them to stay and look at her for as long as they wanted.

Weighing under 5 pounds, I was not allowed to leave the hospital when my mother did. Mildred promised Dr. Twaddle she would leave and directly go to her mother's house to rest. Another white lie occurred. Yes, she did stop and see Lula for a few minutes before having Tup drive her home to the house in Bath.

Dr. Twaddle never found out the difference. Mildred felt just fine. She did have anxiety about the old Boxer dog Darcy around the newborn. What happened next, Mildred swore was a truly sad coincidence. She insisted her entire life the dog had not been harmed by her.

The baby's weight had reached 5 pounds and was scheduled to come home on Tuesday over two weeks since the birth. Late Sunday night, Darcy the dog passed away in his sleep. Tup was upset. Mildred felt sorry for her husband but selfishly she was relieved. On Monday Mildred began altering the baby gowns and dresses she had been given for the baby. Everything was too big for her tiny baby. The cloth diapers had to be folded several times before baby could wear them. Mildred purchased a pair of doll's shoes for her baby's feet. The doll's shoes were the only ones that stayed on the tiny feet. Tup was overjoyed with his daughter. He loved to sit and hold her for hours. Tup joked to his pals that she was the " best thing I ever did and I didn't even know when I did it." At six months old, she giggled all the way as a delighted Tup carried her up to the bathroom in a laundry basket.

At nine months, Mildred did not think her daughter was able to climb the steep stairs to the second floor yet. She did not put a gate across the stairs. One morning after Mildred had finished some kitchen chores, she entered the living room where baby Rhoda had been playing. She discovered the baby was gone. Mildred looked everywhere downstairs. Then she ran upstairs to the large bathroom and three bedrooms.

A large claw foot bathtub sat behind the bathroom door. Mildred opened the door slightly and glanced in, no baby. After another frantic examination of the first floor, Mildred went back up to the second floor. Passing the slightly opened bathroom door, Mildred heard a familiar sound. Her daughter's babbling. This time she went into the bathroom and closed the door behind her. Sure enough, there I was hiding in the small corner between the bathtub and the door.

Mildred quickly bought a child gate to block off those stairs. On sunny days she would walk Rhoda in the carriage the two blocks to the Kennebec Greenhouse to bring Tup lunch. He really enjoyed these visits with his daughter. Once she could stand, Tup stood Rhoda among the many flower varieties like a statue. Rhoda was a crawling one year old when Tup brought home another Boxer dog, he proudly named Darcy II. He promised Mildred to keep the dog at the greenhouse during the day.

Mildred loved bringing Rhoda to Durham to spend time with Lula and Mel. Having grandchildren around lifted their spirits after the house fire. Mel loved holding Rhoda's hand in his as she began to walk around their backyard with cousin Deborah close behind. One of those happy visits happened to be on April 11,1956. A day Mildred will never forget. She described it as the saddest day of her life. That day a freak accident in the mill took her beloved father away forever.

Mildred was devastated and angry. For weeks after the accident she blamed the helper for not having the safety latch on before passing Mel the nail gun. She could not accept the father whom she loved so deeply was dead. A common custom in those days, was to have a family member host the wake. Lula's brother Abner offered to host the wake at his house. Mel's body lay there in Abner's home for three days before the funeral. Although Mel was a member of the Nazarene Church in Lisbon Falls, his funeral was held at the larger Methodist Church nearby. The attendance was massive with many having to stand outside the church.

Members of the Litchfield songsters sang at the service. Mildred wept uncontrollably. Her life would never be the same again. Lula who had lost the only man she had ever loved tried to comfort her distraught daughter. She was a pillar of strength, even at her husband's funeral. Later alone in her bedroom, Lula found it difficult to accept the reality. She held Deborah close to her chest as they cried themselves to sleep. Lula had engraved on Melbourne's headstone, ALL WHO KNEW HIM LOVED HIM. Never a more truer statement. Mildred became deeply depressed. Given the she would have locked herself in her bedroom and wept all day. Melbourne had been a major part of Mildred's life. He was the first man who loved her and she him. She respected and admired her Dad more than any other person. Mildred had to bury her feelings and focus on her own family. Her husband and young child.

The coming days passed quickly as she cared for her growing toddler. In contrast the nights were long and often sleepless ones for Mildred. Her passion for writing poetry emerged significantly. Mildred had been inspired to turn her emotions into sonnets and poems. Her senior year in high school, Mildred wrote and performed the " Class Ode of 1938". She had been happy to write the heartfelt sonnet for her graduation. Mildred was the only birth child of Mel and Lula's to finish high school.

Following the dramatic life changing event penned two poems about her beloved father. The first was called simply My Dad and the second entitled Our Dad. She shared them both with family members.

Mildred continued writing poetry, resulting in a total of 30 poems by the end of her life. Each one inspired by a family member or life altering event. In November 1956, Mildred invited Lula and Deborah to enjoy Thanksgiving at her home in Bath. Notably the first major holiday without Mel. Mildred did her very best to make it a special family day for everyone. Besides a couple of photos from that Thanksgiving Day, I found an audio tape recording. Before Mel's passing, Lula had purchased a reel to reel audio recorder. She felt it important to hold on to family memories. There was a recording of Mel's mother, Delilah Craig reciting a children's story also Lula would bring the audio recorder to church services to record Mel singing hymns, with Mildred accompanying him on the piano or organ.

On that Thanksgiving Day, Lula brought the tape recorder with her to Bath. She asked Mildred to record everyone at the table without telling Tup, Deborah or me. The voices are animated and energetic on the tape. For the next ten years each November, Nana had us listen to those moments on the audio tape recorder. Sadly it turned out to be my father Tup's last Thanksgiving Day with us. This tape recording became a chance for me to hear his distinctive gravelly voice each year. On that recording, I heard my father express his love and sense of humor with me. Two Christmases later in 1958, Lula also purchased an 8 mm movie camera with a hand held light rack.

Lula's children protested this purchase, saying it was unnecessary for a widow on social security to buy such an expensive item. Personally, I am thankful she had the foresight to help preserve our family memories. Unfortunately, those high powered lights were so bright our eyes are squinting or closed on her first attempts at movie making. Over 30 years later, I had them converted to video tapes so we could all enjoy them again.

In the winter of 1957, Mildred and Stan's wife, Beverly decided to visit a fortune teller. Mildred had been to one before therefore she knew about what to expect. This particular fortune teller read palms and tea leaves to predict the future or relive the past. When it came to Mildred's turn the fortune teller asked if she wished to hear about the past or the future. Mildred requested to hear about what the future would have in store for her. The results of the reading confused Mildred. The woman kept telling her, there would be a loss of a special man in Mildred's life. She saw a funeral at a huge church with many flowers and the funeral music would be played on a large pipe organ.

Mildred left quite upset. She believed the fortune teller had told her the past not the future. It seemed like she was told about the loss of her father. There were two clear discrepancies though, Mel's funeral took place in large church not huge and there was no pipe organ. She was indeed correct about lots of flowers.

One evening in March 1957, Mildred walked into the bathroom right after Tup had exited. She was shocked to see blood spots on the floor, in front of the toilet. Mildred questioned Tup about the blood spots. At first he hesitated to answer about where the blood had come from. She persisted until he admitted his urine had been bloody for weeks. Then Tup told Mildred he felt weak and may faint. She noticed his normally ruddy complexion was now very pale. This frightened her. Mildred immediately called for an ambulance.

She grabbed two year old Rhoda, firmly setting her upon the living room sofa. Mildred instructed the child not to move from that spot. Unfortunately, this is one of only two clear memories I have left of my father. My first memory is him dressing me in pajamas as I stood upon the kitchen counter at the house in Bath. Mama told me he did this each night before carrying me up to my crib. My second memory haunted me for years. I kept remembering seeing my father lying down on a board wearing red and white pajamas.

At 10 years old I recalled these memories to Mama. She confirmed both were true experiences. Yes, I had witnessed my father wearing red and white pajamas on the stretcher the night he was taken to the hospital. At the hospital the doctors determined the hemorrhaging was from Tup's liver. His liver had totally deteriorated. Tup had a rare blood type, AB,RH positive. This blood was very scarce. My father had mentioned to Mama when they were dating about the many times he had traveled throughout New England donating blood to others with this rare type.

Now it was he, who needed a blood transfusion. Uncle Abner's wife Rosemond, an RN, ironically had the same blood type. Without hesitation she donated a pint of blood toward my father's fight to live. It was a losing battle. Blood flowed out of Tup's body like water. At one point, Mildred walked into his hospital room shocked to see four IV drip stands surrounding her husband's bed. Both his arms and his feet were attached to an IV. Tup begged Mildred to cover the IV stands because he did not want to watch all four bottles slowly drip blood into his veins. She grabbed four towels from the bathroom to cover up the IV bottles.

The doctor in charge told Mildred the exploratory surgery showed Tup had been sporadically bleeding internally for several years. He asked if she knew of any childhood injuries Tup had experienced. Mildred recalled a story Tup told her about being hit in the face at 16 by a baseball when he was pitching a baseball game. The ball had struck him in the face abruptly knocking him unconscious for several minutes.

When he awoke Tup's parents refused to take him to a doctor. From then on, he never breathed properly through his nose. He joined the Army in WWII, serving in Japan. Like many young men in the service, Tup began heavily drinking alcohol. Each night before bed, he would place a dap of Vicks vapor rub on the tip of his nose. He told Mildred it was the only way he could breathe at night. Tup told her about the daily stomach pains that bothered him. Of course his first cure to deaden the pain was a drink of alcohol.

Upon hearing these recollections, his doctor was convinced the broken nose injury had started blood dripping into his esophagus eventually into his liver.

Over the years, with the addition of alcohol, the blood led to rapid to his liver deterioration. My father never realized the severity of his condition. Mama and the doctors let him think he was healing. He would joke to his visitors about having a big coming home party upon his release from the hospital. For six weeks Tup lay in that hospital bed. He talked to Rhoda on the phone almost every day. He would tell me, " Papa will be home real soon." Phone calls I cannot remember. Even at 2 years old, I knew how to play my parents against each other. If my father asked who I loved, I would say," Papa, Mama" but if my mother asked who I loved I would reply " Mama, Papa."

Mama told me, he prompted that response in his final phone conversation with me. Mildred started preparing for Tup's eminent death. His doctors diagnosis was terminal from day one. Back in 1957 there were no procedures to repair or replace a human liver. Mildred was going to lose Tup.

Last April, she had lost her father, this April it was to be her husband. On April 29th 1957 at the age of 38, Thornton (Tup) Gray Henderson died. My father's funeral was held in Bath's largest church. His brother filled the church with an abundance of flowers from the greenhouse. Relatives took care of little Rhoda while Mildred attended the funeral service. About an hour into the funeral service the huge pipe organ covered with flowers began to play a hymn. Suddenly, Mildred felt chills up and down her spine.

She realized the fortune teller had indeed told Mildred what her future would hold. It was Tup's death she had predicted.

CHAPTER THIRTEEN

Just Us

MILDRED insisted on her husband being buried at the cemetery in Lisbon Falls near her father. This upset Tup's family who all lived in Bath. They wanted him buried there instead. Two days after the funeral Tup's father Charles gave Mildred more bad news. The house in Bath Charles's house, the one we had been living in, was being sold. Rhoda and her had to move out immediately. This was the first time we were homeless. Mildred frantically called her uncle Abner. She asked if her former apartment on Spring St., Lisbon Falls, where she had operated Mildred's Beauty Shop, was available.

Abner said it would not be ready for a few weeks. He did own an apartment house two blocks away from Spring St. that she could rent in the meantime. The majority of furnishings at the Bath house were not considered Mildred's. She had only a bed, bureau and clothes to pack. One item she wanted to bring was Tup's 5 gallon glass jar. The jar was stored in a safe in the basement. Every evening when Tup came home from work he would empty the change from his pockets into the jar.

He had called it Rhoda's jar. Tup and Mildred had decided once it was full, they could start me a savings account. On the last day at the house in Bath, Mildred went down to retrieve Rhoda's jar. It was gone ! Where was Rhoda's jar?

She immediately called her father -in-law Charles to inquire about the change jar. Charles assured Mildred he would find the change jar. That evening Charles came to the house with the glass change jar in hand. Tup's brother Melvin had taken the change jar to the greenhouse.

Apparently, he was unaware who the contents belonged to. The amount contained in the change jar totaled fifty dollars. Mama started a savings account for me with it at a Lisbon Falls bank. The balance stayed at fifty for over a year. As relatives sent me $2.00 or $5.00 in birthday cards or Christmas cards, it began to grow. Mama suggested I deposit half of whatever amount of money I received. Tup had told Mildred he had invested money into the greenhouse after returning from the service. Mildred was never compensated for this investment.

At eighteen I was surprised to get a call from my uncle Melvin. Since my father's death his family had only contacted me twice. Grandfather Charles came to call on me, when I was ten years old. He stayed about an hour. My father's other brother Fred visited me at Nana's house the following summer. Fred talked to me through the screen door for 15 minutes. Melvin had called to ask a favor of me. He wanted me to sign off as Tup's surviving heir on a land inheritance from an Aunt.

Against Mama's wishes, I signed the agreement he sent me. I did not want to start trouble with my father's family. Two decades later, after Mama had passed, Melvin sent me a sympathy card with a copy of the Henderson family tree. A Henderson reunion had been held, I was not invited. To commemorate the reunion, a booklet of the Henderson family tree was printed. I found it quite peculiar that my mother and I were excluded from it. The tree acknowledged my father's first marriage, divorce and his death. No mention of his second marriage or his daughter!

In spite of being left out or perhaps because of the fact, I wanted to attend Melvin's funeral in 1994 in Bath. Melvin had been murdered by a former greenhouse employee. He had been targeted because he was gay. At the funeral I finally met many of the Henderson relatives, thirty-seven years after my father's death. Awkward and at times uncomfortable, we spoke in small talk conversations.

Of course, they thought I looked exactly like Tup. Another shocker came months after Melvin's death. I received a letter from his lawyer. Melvin had actually bequeathed me five thousand dollars in his will. Was it payback for Tup's investment or a thank you for signing off on the land agreement.

In late summer of 1957, Mildred and Rhoda moved into the second floor apartment on Spring St. in Lisbon Falls. The former home of Mildred's Beauty Shop. Uncle Bob was still living in the first floor apartment. Since his divorce, Bob lived there alone. Now a widow, Mildred relied solely on her social security and Tup's VA check. These two monthly checks totaled two hundred dollars. Mildred had a substantial hospital bill to pay from Tup's illness. He did not have medical insurance.

In the 50's, there were no daycare services. She couldn't leave Rhoda to go to work. Lula in her late fifties was raising Deborah and Mildred did not want to burden her with another small child. I remember the once a month shopping trips to the grocery store. Mama kept a tight budget. The two hundred a month had to pay for food, rent, gas for the car, utilities and of course the hospital bill.

Every Sunday, we joined Deborah and Nana for Sunday Dinner. Either Lula or Mildred would provide the entrée, usually meat or chicken, depending on who had more money that week. The other one supplied vegetables and dessert. At the end of the month they sometimes had to borrow from each other to make it through until the next check came. The main dish for Sunday dinners varied each week, a beef roast, baked chicken or meatloaf.

We divided the leftovers. The leftovers could feed us for another two or three days. During those years Mama and I ate a lot of soups, casseroles and spaghetti. A filling meal which produced good leftovers.

On Rhoda's fifth birthday, Mildred gave her a calico kitten. Rhoda named her Penny. It was to replace her cat Angel Face. Angel Face had been killed by a stray dog at Lula's house in Durham. Uncle Bob did not like cats. Mildred tried keeping Penny confined inside the apartment. One day Penny snuck out. She ran down our stairs and out the front door of the apartment building. Once outside, Penny climbed the tall oak tree nearby. When Mildred and Rhoda discovered Penny the cat was missing, they asked Bob if he had seen the cat. He mentioned seeing the cat run out the door. Rhoda and Mildred quickly went outside. Penny was heard crying high up in the oak tree.

Rhoda began to cry too. Mildred knew there was no way she could reach the cat. She called a friend, who happened to be a volunteer fire-fighter. Mildred asked him if the fire department could help get the cat down from the oak tree. In less than 2 minutes the ladder truck came roaring up Spring Street with sirens blazing.

People on Spring St. and surrounding streets came running out to see where the fire was. Mildred's friend driving the firetruck thought it would be fun to turn on the siren. One fireman positioned the ladder against the oak tree. He slowly climbed up to retrieve the cat. A scared Penny hissed at him and left a few scratches on his arm. As he handed the cat over to a teary eyed Rhoda all was forgiven. Penny never escaped out that door again.

The cat escapade paled in comparison to the event which took place the following Saturday evening. Mildred and her daughter shared a bed in their small apartment. Mildred was awakened by loud voices and constant pounding on her apartment door. She carefully slipped out of bed, as not to wake Rhoda. When Mildred approached the locked door the voices became louder. Mildred asked,"who's there ?" One voice yelled back, " Where's Bob ?" through the four paneled wooden door. Mildred shouted back that he was not here. She told them this was the wrong apartment.

Mildred said Bob lived on the first floor. Suddenly, the perpetrators began kicking the bottom panels of the door. Mildred watched in horror as pieces of the wooden panels fell inside onto her floor. She ran quickly back to the bedroom. Mildred wrapped the bedspread around her sleepy child. She scooped the child up into her arms and carried her daughter down the back stairs and ran out the backdoor. Mildred never stopped to look back in the darkness,

Mildred ran across the street to her Aunt Verda's house. She began frantically pounding on Verda's front door. Several lights appeared in Verda's house. A pair of drowsy eyes peered out from behind a sheer curtain in the front window. The scared eyes were trying to see who had awakened them at 2 a.m.

When Verda saw it was Mildred carrying Rhoda, she immediately opened the front door. I vaguely recall Mama plopping me down on the overstuffed chair in Verda's dining room. Verda's husband and her two teenage children stood before me, staring into my frightened face. My mother called the police who responded very quickly.

We waited for nearly two hours at Verda's house. Finally the police said it was safe to return to our apartment. The sun was rising as we made our way back inside the building. The smell of booze was overwhelming. We entered carefully, dodging broken glass. Whiskey and beer bottles lined the second floor stairs leading to our apartment. Mildred saw that two bottom panels of her apartment door had been totally destroyed. Bob came up to apologize to Mildred that afternoon. The intruders, two men and one woman were drinking buddies of Bob's. They came collect money Bob owed them. Overnight in a jail cell sobered them up. No charges were filed against them. Bob helped us clean up the mess on the stairs and in the hallway.

My cousin Deborah was already enrolled in the Lisbon Falls school system, when I started Sub-Primary (now called kindergarten) in 1959. No bus service meant Nana had to drive her every day to our apartment in Lisbon Falls from Durham. The town of Durham was in the process of building an elementary school. This new elementary school would replace several one room schoolhouses spread across the rural town of Durham.

Our apartment was three blocks from the Marion T. Morse Elementary School. Deb and I started walking to school with other neighborhood children. On a crisp autumn afternoon in October 1960 as Deb and I were walking home from school, we encountered a strange incident. She was nine and I was six years old. Being a first grader, I loved to scuff my feet through the leaves gathered along the sidewalks. Deb was first to see the car approaching. I always kept my head down while walking therefore I didn't notice the car. A large dark colored car slowly followed us as we walked up the hill on High Street. After Deb turned and looked at the car, it sped up passing us.

At the top of the hill the car made a U-turn and slowly drove back towards us again. Deb became uneasy about the situation. She grabbed my and shouted, " Let's run." Being six years old and loving to run, I took this as a challenge to beat my older cousin home.

We turned onto Spring Street heading toward my apartment building. Mama was waiting for us on the front steps. Deb burst into tears. She told Mama about the car and how afraid she was. I had been totally oblivious of the car. Hearing Deb's shaky voice explain what happened, I systematically began to cry too.

Mama took us inside and calmed us down. She tried to get a description of the car from Deb. All Deb could remember was that the car was big and dark colored. Mama had to drive Deborah back to Nana's house in Durham anyway so we first drove around the streets in Lisbon Falls looking for the car that had followed us. We never found it. We couldn't prove whether this vehicle meant us any harm. It was a small Maine town in the 60's, children were presumed safe here. At least that is what I thought.

A couple years later, I heard a conversation in Nana's living room, putting me in a more cautious frame of mind. Mama, Nana and my 16 year old cousin Craig were having an intense discussion. A frightening occurrence had taken place in Lisbon Falls that week involving a six year old girl. Craig was fuming mad because his half-sister was the same age and living in Lisbon Falls. The little girl had become separated from her classmates while walking home from school. An hour later she was found walking near her home holding bloody underpants.

The little girl told her parents and the local sheriff she knew the boys who " hurt " her. They were boys in her neighborhood. She even told their names. Unfortunately, this little girl was characterized as mentally challenged and wore very thick eye glasses. The authorities did not believe her story. Nothing was ever done to the boys. It was again the 1960's where children were to be seen and not heard.

CHAPTER FOURTEEN

COUNTRY LIVING

MILDRED was anxious to return to rural Durham to live. The new elementary school was completed. Deb would be attending in the fall. Mildred asked her mother if she could have the former garage, now partial house that Stanley had briefly lived in. Lula agreed to deed over the one acre of land where the building sat to Mildred. She was happy to finally own land in her hometown of Durham. The fact the building was in need of major repairs did not discourage Mildred at all. Each month a portion of her Social Security check was taken to purchase building materials from a local lumber store. One month it might be the purchase of a couple sheets of sheetrock, the next month a bundle of roof shingles and so on.

Each day after taking Rhoda to school, Mildred drove to Durham to work on her future home. Sometimes on the weekend, her cousin Dale, Uncle Bob's son, came to help her with the construction. Luckily Lula's new neighbor, Mr. Harlow Tucker, was a retired master carpenter from New York. He and his wife had moved to Maine to enjoy their golden years. Seeing Mildred struggling with the renovations drew Mr. Tucker back to his trade.

Mr. Tucker was in his late seventies and had out lived four previous wives. Physically he had to use a cane to walk but mentally he was still sharp as a tack. Mr. Tucker gave Mildred step by step instructions to help her turn the former garage into a livable house.

Mr. Tucker watched from a lawn chair as Mildred shingled the roof according to his directions. I can see him now, pointing with his cane and telling Mama where to begin the starter shingles. Once the roof was complete, Mr. Tucker instructed her on how to put the cedar shingles on the main house. Mildred's Uncle Woodrow, her father's younger brother was an electrician. He offered to do all the rewiring for her. In the fall of 1962 we had to vacate our apartment. Again we were looking for a home. Just like when we had to leave Bath after my father died. This time her recently widowed Aunt May was moving back to Maine from Boston and needed a place to live. Abner told Mildred he had promised May the apartment on Spring Street while she searched for a house to buy. He had believed we would living in Durham by then. The building in Durham was not move in ready for another couple of months.

The oil tank had to be hooked up to the stove. An old hand dug well had to be primed. Windows and a front door had not been installed. Nana told Mama we could stay with her and Deborah until the house was ready to move into. We brought our few belongings with us to Nana's house in October.

My mother was anxious to be in our house by Christmas. She was given old used doors and windows from friends who were replacing theirs. She hurriedly completed all the necessary construction needs by the last week of November. Mildred's goal was achieved. We moved in before the holiday season. Mildred finally had her own house, a home of her own. She vowed never to be in a homeless situation again.

Our first couple of winters in the Durham house were really rough. The old wooden door used as the entrance failed as a barrier from winter weather. It revealed a multitude of significant cracks and severe imperfections. Each time snow came at night, we woke up to find a substantial snow drift INSIDE the kitchen. The door's porous surface resulted in major drafts. Preceding a forecasted snowstorm, Mildred stuffed pieces of cloth around the doorframe. She would also duct tape plastic over the door panels inside. By the second winter Mildred had installed an aluminum storm door in front of the old drafty wooden one.

Our heat source came from a second hand combination gas cook stove and oil burner. The large appliance occupied two-thirds of our small kitchen space. Mildred was simply grateful to have it. The house floor plan was basically two 18 feet long by 12 feet wide rooms divided by a wall.

Each room had multiple functions. Talk about your open floor plans. The kitchen, living room dining area and bathroom dominated one room. The second room separated by a sliding wooden door accommodated our sleeping and storage area. Mama's double bed at one end of the room and my twin size bed at the other end.

Positioned off the kitchen another sliding door covered the 5x5 foot boxed in bathroom. A toilet paper holder attached inside the door, positioned at the correct height when closed, was an ingenious idea. The bathroom consisted of a toilet, wall hung medicine cabinet and a five foot white cast iron bathtub setting on blocks. The raised tub gave Mildred 6 inches of storage underneath for extra toilet paper rolls, a toilet brush, extra soap, a wash basin and a few cleaning products.

To hide these items from view, Mildred attached a 5 ft. x 6 in. piece of pegboard with small magnets that clung to the tub plus a chrome handle for easy flip up access. Unable to afford a hot water heater, we only had cold water piped into the bathtub. In the winter a kettle always sat on the oil burner side of the combo stove, which meant we had continuous hot water available for bathing. In summer, the kettle was used on the gas stove to heat water when needed.

A Rubbermaid basin was used daily for sponge baths. Another plastic basin in the kitchen was used to wash the dishes in. Compact living conditions inspired Mama to use her New England ingenuity. The small kitchen area plus the lack of wooden support behind the walls, did not allow for any kitchen wall cabinets.

Mildred purchased a tall metal hutch for her dishes, pots and utensils. Next, she took four 2x4 inch planks, a few strapping boards, a metal handle and a couple chair casters and build herself a sliding pantry. The pantry fit snuggly in the 6 inch gap between the stove combo and the half wall divider that separated the kitchen and living room.

The pantry was the perfect size to hold cans and boxed gelatin packages. On the other side of the half wall, Mama securely fastened a table leaf from an old chrome legged, Formica topped kitchen table someone had thrown out. Just big enough for two stools to set for Mama and me. A second hand Philco refrigerator kept our food cold. The freezer section froze meats, chicken or ice cubes but never ice cream.

Arranged in the living room area was a 13 inch. B&W television set on a two foot corner stand. An old four foot two cushion sofa and a pedestal ashtray. Mildred's budget included Tup's $5400 hospital bill, electricity bill, oil bill, property taxes and groceries. A bigger television was not a priority.

Unfortunately, Mama was addicted to nicotine. A pack of Pall Mall cigarettes cost 33 cents. Smoking half a pack each day took a chunk out of her budget. She and Idolyne, a smoker too, tried to be thrifty with their nicotine habit. A habit certainly not learned from Lula and Mel. They never smoked or drank alcohol. Idolyne knew a friend who owned a smoke shop. She purchased bags of loose tobacco, tissue papers and a metal gadget to cleverly roll these elements into cigarettes. My cousins and I took foolish pride in learning to operate this gadget. Several attempts later we managed to roll some decent cigarettes. Years later, watching my mother suffering from the results of those damn cigarettes, I felt guilty enabling Mama by rolling cigarettes or purchasing them for her. In the 60's, a kid was never questioned when purchasing packs of Pall Malls at the local market.

Mama sent me in with a dollar to buy her three packs. The store clerk, a non-smoker, knew how unhealthy they were. He would lecture me about the certain death sentence they provoked. What was I to do? I was an obedient nine year old. Anytime I questioned her judgement I was given the same reply," Do as I say, not as I do." a common motherly quote.

This quote was exercised often when subjects like alcohol, cigarettes or sex was mentioned. Apparently, my Nana had not accentuated its meaning to her offspring as often. They totally dismissed her, seeing as they all smoked, drank and had pre-marital sex. The three vices Nana had abstained from.

The oil burner kept the kitchen, living room and bathroom area warm. With the wooden sliding door separating the bedrooms closed, the bedrooms had no heat source. Layers and layers of heavy blankets became the answer to keeping Mama and I warm in the winter months. Mama promised me my own bedroom before I turned 10 years old. She kept her promise. In 1964 her cousin Dale helped her build a six foot by twelve foot addition to the house. The addition included my bedroom and a storage room. The fact I had to walk through Mama's bedroom to reach mine didn't bother me.

A cheap bamboo bi-fold door was hung to separate the two bedrooms. I even had a small walk-in closet and a window. Sure, the old wooden nine panel window needed caulking, the sash did not open and the sill was cracked but I still felt privileged to have a window. Unfortunately, without heat in the bedrooms during winter, my window became heavily coated, INSIDE, with 2 inches of frosted ice crystals. On Christmas that year my favorite present was an electric blanket. It kept me so warm. Complaining was not an option, I felt lucky to have a house to live in.

Mildred looked for part time jobs outside the home. Her income existed of her social security check and Tup's veteran's check. Both checks combined total was about $275 a month. She started accepting temporary employment in various places to supplement her income. According to federal guidelines and restrictions, she would lose her social security income if her extra earnings were over $650 a year. Mama agreed I was responsible enough to stay home alone after school until she arrived home from her job. A regular latchkey kid.

Mama found a job as inspection picker at Worumbo woolen mill a mile away in Lisbon Falls. Her first real job in over 10 years. Mama was required to stand for 8-9 hours a day in front of long sheets of woolen cloth under bright florescent lights to inspect the cloth for rogue pieces of thread or yarns. Her task was to remove these unwanted threads with a small pair of tweezers. The extra money allowed Mama to purchase cheap wood paneling to cover my bedroom walls plus a green shag area rug to cover the plywood floor. She bought two unfinished chest of drawers. She stained them and the bamboo folding doors green. I completed my décor with two hot pink foot-shaped shag rugs.

Next, I strung 8 strings of multi-colored beads on a tension rod to separate the bed section from the three foot vanity section. My vanity was an old painted shelf below a wall hung mirror. Mama covered a small wooden barrel for my vanity stool. It worked for me! Torn out pages from 16 magazine featuring the Beatles taped on the walls served as posters. After all it was the 1960s.

Those two hours I was home alone each day was just the right amount of time for me to do homework, start dinner and watch Dark Shadows on our 13 inch black and white television. My most memorable Christmas came in 1968. Mama saved enough to buy one big present. A 21 inch Admiral console Color television set. Wow! She even bought the outside tv antenna which she attached on the roof herself. Of course, it took several tries before all three channels were adjusted to the correct color. For the first time we were able to see Dorothy arrive in living color in the Land of Oz. The Wizard of Oz was a favorite of mine. We also enjoyed watching the old Shirley Temple musicals.

A few months later, Mildred bought more wood paneling for the living room and kitchen area. The paneling covered the dingy, smokey wallpapered walls. Mildred's clever idea to make the room look larger was to glue two rows of 12 inch square mirror tiles from ceiling to floor on the back living room wall. The elusion worked. People entering the front door into the kitchen looking straight ahead believed the house extended further than it did. This effect created a special impression during the Christmas holiday. A scrawny three-sided evergreen placed before the mirrored wall transformed it into a beautiful full tree.

Money was always tight. We had the necessities like food, clothing, heat and a car for transportation. Our driveway was 750 feet long. A weekly two foot snowstorm in winter could cause problems.

If Mildred did not have the $10. to pay someone to plow the driveway, she would have to shovel it herself. She was always fearful of a house fire or a medical emergency and wanted to keep the driveway cleared to guarantee a fire truck or ambulance could reach our house.

The shoveling process depended on the type of snow. If it was light, fluffy snow a path the width of a car could be shoveled in a couple of hours. A heavy wet snow took Mildred an entire day of shoveling. She would start in the early morning and not stop until dusk. This of course was when she was not working. When she worked and there was a major snowstorm, Mildred preferred to walk the mile to work. Driving in snowstorms made her extremely nervous. Not having a telephone in our house was especially difficult during snowstorms. Deborah and I would use walkie talkies we received one Christmas to communicate between our house and Nana's. I was a sophomore in high school when our telephone was installed.

Mama felt with Nana's increasing age and her diabetes, investing in a telephone was the right move. She wanted Nana to be able to contact her if a health emergency occurred. Mama even paid extra for a private line instead of a party line with multiple users.

The seventies brought many changes. Mildred's part time job at the woolen mill ceased. She found some unusual jobs to earn extra money. Mildred accepted a six week long job from a car dealership to prepare dirty used cars for selling. Exteriors were washed and waxed and interiors were scrubbed and vacuumed.

I offered to bring in extra money by ironing people's laundry. The only two clients I had were Aunt Verda and Mama's good friend Lucy, who each week dropped off a basket of wrinkled items for me to iron. We agreed on two dollars per basket was a fair payment.

Aunt Verda's laundry basket usually consisted of blouses, linen towels and tablecloths. Lucy brought blouses, aprons and her husband Eddie's boxer shorts. Lucy also sent a can of spray starch along with her wrinkled clothes. She asked me to spray the blouses and aprons with the spray starch to make them crisp, allowing water and dirt to roll off easier. With no men in my household, I had never seen men's boxers before. After I spray starched Lucy's blouses and aprons, I proceeded to spray Eddie's boxers. The whole basket looked smooth and crisp when I sent it back to Lucy.

Mama received a call the next day. I heard her laughing with the caller. After hanging up the phone, she told me the caller had been Lucy. She was pleased with the ironing I had done but husband Eddie said to tell me next time don't spray starch his boxers. He was very chafe from the stiffness irritating his private parts. I felt so embarrassed and stupid. I never did that again.

The 1970's changed Mildred's life dramatically. She applied for the dispatcher position at the Town of Lisbon's Senior Citizens minibus service. It was called a minibus but was really a large fifteen passenger van. Mildred wanted a full time occupation. No more part time jobs that did not offer health insurance of benefits. She loved being dispatcher. Her office was located in the Town Office building on main street in Lisbon Falls, still just a mile a commute.

Ironically, the job reunited Mildred with many former beauty shop customers. The free bus rides were sponsored by the town and had only one requirement. A rider had to be a minimum 55 years of age and live in the town. Fifty-five year old seniors could travel to medical appointments, hair salons or shopping centers within a 15 mile radius for free.

Mildred's new co-workers happily embraced her with open arms. Some becoming really close friends with her. Mama watched proudly as I graduated from Lisbon High School in 1972. I realized our financial situation would not allow me to attend college. Mama supported my decision to take a full time office position at the LLBean Inc. complex in nearby Freeport.

We both received the minimum wage of $1.80 an hour, for our jobs. Mama and I agreed on me paying $25.00 a month for living expenses. The payment included utilities, food and laundromat costs. A hand dug well and no water heater meant no washing machine in the house. A clothes line behind the house was our dryer. The hot summers would often cause Nana's well to become bone dry. We did our best to conserve water during the hot summer months. Finally, Nana decided to have an artisan well drilled. She was astounded when the well company told her they had discovered a " lake of water" underground expelling 90 gallons a minute. Lula never had to worry about her well going dry ever again.

New life changes evolved quickly for Mildred. A blind date for Rhoda with John Demchak led to love and a subsequent engagement. Surprisingly, John was the nephew of Lina one of Mildred's best friends in school. For years, Lina had encouraged Mildred to date her brother and later her brother -in – law because she desperately wanted Mildred as a sister. When hearing about Rhoda and John, Lina joked how it took another generation before Mildred was part of her family. Everyone was delighted about the upcoming nuptials. Lula offered her granddaughter the parcel of land between her house and Mildred's. The former site of the burned farmhouse.

One major stipulation towards ownership was that John and Rhoda had to build a new driveway to access Lula's house. Lula had been using the shortcut from Mildred's driveway to reach her raised ranch style house. She could no longer climb the steep front stairs to enter the house. Once the new driveway was completed Lula signed over the land. The shortcut became Rhoda and John's front lawn.

Construction took two years and all the couple's savings. A small wedding was planned for the summer of 1977. Mildred was pleased to have her only child living right next door. For twenty years it had been just the two of them, depending on one another in that small house. Mildred had not lived alone since marrying Tup. Mildred strongly suggested she be the one to walk Rhoda down the aisle on her wedding day. Rhoda wanted a more traditional manner and asked her cousin Craig to do the honors. Sometimes I regret not let Mama walk me down the aisle that day. Respectfully when the minister asked the question, who gives this woman to marry this man, Craig replied" her mother does." Craig and wife Lynn offered to host a honeymoon trip at their lovely home in Arlington, Virginia.

Craig worked as a Secret Service Agent in the White House in Washington D.C. Lynn, worked in a division of the CIA in Washington D.C The newlyweds enjoyed visiting the tourist sites in Washington D.C. Craig and Lynn were generous hosts taking them to plays at the Kennedy Center and making sure their stay was a pleasant one.

At 56, Mildred liked her minibus dispatcher position but hoped to retire at age 62. She felt she wanted to be young enough to spoil any future grandchildren. The latter wish came sooner than expected. Nine months plus two weeks from the honeymoon, Rhoda gave birth to a beautiful baby girl. They jokingly called her the honeymoon baby. Mildred and Lula were thrilled to celebrate Mother's Day in 1978 with a five day old granddaughter and great-granddaughter respectively.

Rhoda's husband John, was head electrician at the nearby paper mill in Pejepscot, Maine. A few weeks into their marriage, John was given a promotion. Finances increased allowing Rhoda to stay home with the baby. Mildred became new Nana and Lula was referred to a old Nana. Living a ball toss away, enabled Mildred to be a frequent visitor. Each day after work she would stop by to see the baby. Lula loved the many times Rhoda brought the baby down the path between the two houses for an afternoon visit.

Just a toddler when Grampa Mel died, Nana was the only grandparent I had ever known or shared my life with. For 24 years I had lived a few yards away from her. Nana's house provided a comforting atmosphere for all her grandchildren. Like the popular quote states, IF MAMA SAYS NO, ASK GRANDMA," or in my case it was ask Nana.

She could pull a loose tooth with ease, distracting your pain by talking about your pets or school. She could whip up your favorite dessert as she told you stories about her own childhood.

Nana's patience with us was admirable. Teaching us baking skills, as we turned her kitchen into chaos. The conversations she shared about her life experiences are moments I will never forget. Nana's common sense knowledge and practical wisdom went beyond her eighth grade level education. As Nana's health declined, the fear of living her last days in a nursing home began to dominated her thoughts. Nana started expressing daily, how she needed to sell land to pay for any nursing home facility. We tried to reassure Nana the nursing home anxiety was unfounded. She still worried it was going to happen. That was why my husband and I took out a mortgage to purchase seven acres of the land she inherited from John Patrick. Our offer immediately relieved her worries.

Sadly, Nana never received the money from the land sale. She passed away one week before being able to cash the bank check. The check, car and her house went directly into Nana's estate. Six months later the estate was totally finalized. Lula's assets were to be divided equally among all her heirs. Tragically, five months after Lula's death, daughter Idolyne died of a sudden massive heart attack as only fifty-four years old.

Stanley and Mildred were heartbroken from losing their mother in June 1979 and then their sister in November 1979. Eventually, Lula's assets were divided among Mildred, Stanley, adopted granddaughter Deborah and Idolyne's three children. Nana's family bible and some of her braided rugs are the items I received and cherish. Idolyne's sudden death brought back heartbreaking memories of Mel's death, leaving Mildred shattered.

A second granddaughter and a demanding work schedule were welcomed diversions at this time in Mildred's life. Although she loved her job and her co-workers, retiring at sixty-two remained her goal. She was anxiously looking forward to spending more time with her grandchildren. Since their births, Mildred had obeyed her daughter and son-in-law's wishes that she not smoke around the grandchildren. Both John's parents had quit before their first granddaughter was born. Being the 1980's Mildred's workplace permitted smoking. She smoked at the office, in her car and in her home.

Living alone also fostered poor diet choices. Mildred justified skipping meals with the excuse about not having to cook a meal for just one. Instead of eating healthy foods in her diet, she substituted a cigarette. Many weeknights her good friend Lucy, a chain smoker, came to Mildred's to play the board game, Scrabble. Each smoke-filled evening lasting a minimum of 3 hours.

Exercise became the walk between our houses to visit the granddaughters. In 1983 her co-workers began planning a surprise retirement party as Mildred approached age 62. Friends, family members and all her co-workers attended the party. Her five year old granddaughter was coaxed into singing Mildred's favorite song, "You Are My Sunshine" before the crowd. Mildred loved it. Two male co-workers, dressed as the Chippendale Dancers, presented Mildred with a large cake. Mildred called the party a total success.

Retirement allowed for new opportunities. Mildred joined Lucy on scenic bus trips to Northern Maine and Boston. Her Aunt Verda, diagnosed with MS now resided in an Auburn nursing home facility ten miles away. Mildred's free time allowed her to make frequent visits to visit with her Aunt. Late Summer 1985, I announced my third pregnancy. Mama was excited to meet her new grandchild. She immediately began crocheting a bonnet and booties set. Ultrasound/sonograms procedures were not commonplace at the time. We did not have the privilege to find out what the gender was. Mama trimmed the white baby set with a neutral yellow ribbon. The first two grandchildren had received white baby sets with white ribbon which she changed to pink ribbon once the girls were born.

Mildred disregarded any health warnings. She made excuses for her constant flushed face after doing light housework or the dizziness following her mowing the grass. Poor diet, heavy smoking plus no exercise led to severe health issues.

Eloise her cousin was an RN, every time she saw Mama, she commented on her sweaty red face. Nurse Eloise would bring out her stethoscope and blood pressure cuff. The procedure revealed each time dangerously high numbers concluding Mama was at risk for a stroke or heart attack. Mama's refusal to get a checkup stemmed from pure fear. She feared what the results would show. Mama had not seen a doctor since my birth, over 31 years. Self- diagnosis and self-medication became her answer. Colds or flu solutions were simple bed rest and chicken noodle soup.

She refused to take aspirin for headaches or pain relief. I recall an incident where Mama slipped in the winter, on an icy spot in our driveway and fell down hard. She was only wearing slippers and a robe. Inside the pocket of the robe were two very sharp crochet needles. One needle actually penetrated her skin, piercing a two inch hole in Mama's stomach. Bloody and faint, she refused to see a doctor. Mama simply dosed herself with hydrogen peroxide and covered the wound with a band aid. She considered her own health a low priority. Mama began continuously worrying about her aunt Verda.

The numbness in Verda's legs once misdiagnosed as a pinched nerve was determined to be MS. Her children decided to send her to a nursing home facility. She became wheelchair bound. Mama strongly disliked nursing homes. Nonetheless, she put on a smile when visiting her aunt. Unfortunately, the visits took an emotional and physical toll on Mama. In early September 1985, Mama took her great nephew and her second granddaughter to visit Aunt Verda at the nursing home. Mama usually came back depressed and physically unsettled. It was hard for Mama to see her aunt in that kind of circumstance.

CHAPTER FIFTEEN

Goodbye Is Not Easy

ON the drive home that day, Mama narrowly missed a head on collision with a distracted driver. The incident was very upsetting to her. Our two houses stood 50 feet apart from each other. Seeing Mama pull into her driveway, I walked from my house over to retrieve my daughter. Mama had taken her nephew home already. As she stepped from her car, Mama's appearance startled me. Her face was sweaty and flushed. Her hands trembling.

Before I was given a chance to ask, Mama erupted into an emotional outburst about the near miss accident. It took several minutes to calm her down. We spoke about her visit with Aunt Verda. Mama declared she would prefer death rather than live under those conditions. These were remarks I had heard many times before.

My four year old daughter and I walked back to our house. Mama walked very slowly to her house and went inside. Everything changed from that moment on. Apparently that evening, Mama felt a sharp pain on the right side of her chest. She dismissed it as indigestion. A false belief that only left side pains are related to the heart is a dangerous one, especially in women. Heart disease is the number one killer of women.

Often in women, the chest pains are mistaken as indigestion. Idolyne believed it to be indigestion as well when she was had her massive heart attack. The intense pain kept Mama awake all night. In the morning I walked over to see her. Finding her still in bed at 10 a.m. was a total shock. Mama then told me about her sleepless night. She explained it was due to pains in her chest and back.

Self- diagnosing the problem as a flu bug or an illness she acquired from the nursing home visit, Mama complained about a nagging cough and nausea. I began to worry about her condition. Later in the day, I brought her chicken noodle soup and a bottle of ginger ale. She had requested the ginger ale, hoping it would settle her stomach. Mama promised me she'd rest in bed. I told her to call if she needed help. At 8 a.m. the next morning I was surprised to see her standing at my back door dressed in her best outfit with full makeup on. Before I could ask her anything Mama reminded me that it was Deborah's birthday. Then Mama told me it was free cheese and rice day for seniors at the Lisbon Town Office.

Absorbing these immaterial statements, from someone who was bedridden the previous day I found quite bizarre. Mama said she felt weak and wanted me to go get the free cheese for her. I asked her why she was out of bed after being so ill twenty-four hours earlier. Mama did not respond to my question.

She started repeating over and over again about the day being Deborah's birthday. My gut told me something was terribly wrong here ! Was she having a stroke ? Dementia ? What was happening ? Taking her hand, I walked a wobbly Mama back to her house and helped her back into her bed. The lipstick and face powder had failed to conceal her ashen skin color or glazed eyes.

Once she was settled back in bed, I ran back to my house and told John what had just happened. He urged me to call an ambulance. He thought it could be a stroke. I knew she would never agree to an ambulance being called. I called her friend Lucy and explained the situation. If anyone could convince Mama to go to the hospital it was Lucy. Lucy arrived at Mama's house in 5 minutes. John said he'd watch the girls while Lucy and I took Mama to the hospital.

We went inside Mama's house to convince her to go to the hospital. Seeing her shaky and having to crawl out of bed elevated our mission. Her right leg from foot to knee was not turning a dark purplish gray. I had seen this happen to my Nana. This meant blood circulation in her leg had stopped. Diabetes had caused Nana's leg to go black. What was causing this ? As we expected, Mama refused an ambulance. She did concede to have Lucy drive her to the hospital emergency room.

We helped her into the front seat of Lucy's car. I quickly settled into the backseat. Lucy drove the 20 minutes to Parkview Hospital in Brunswick. We stayed for three hours while the emergency staff examined Mama. The emergency room doctor eventually admitted her for tests.

The doctor was amazed to hear that Mama had not seen a medical physician for over 30 years. The following three days were hectic. I went to the hospital every day to check on Mama's condition. She was given an EKG and other tests to determine her condition.

Mama was more coherent. She had stopped repeating herself. Every time I left, she kept insisting that I didn't need to come back each day. Mama demanded I get more rest because I was pregnant. She told me my girls needed me more than she did. I ignored her pleas.

The fact a hurricane was impacting Maine at this time was not helping. Hospital visiting hours ended at 8p.m. Consequently, I drove home amidst heavy rains and high winds each night. At 1 a.m. on the third night of Mama's hospitalization, I received a phone call from her attending physician.

Following an exploratory surgery, he wanted to transport Mama to Maine Medical Center in Portland for more extensive tests. Her condition had gotten much worse. They had no solid answers about her illness. I never went back to sleep after that call. John drove me to Portland in the morning. His parents offered to watch our children for the day.

It was an anxious ride to Portland. The hurricane was at its peak stage. That day was a turning point for me as well. Mama's independence I had witnessed my entire life was diminished when I saw the tubes pumping oxygen in her nostrils and an endotracheal tube in her throat. Mama begged the nurse to remove the throat tube. The nurse finally removed it. Our visit was rather brief. Our visit was rather brief. As we stood there talking to Mama we could hear the hurricane raging outside. Hospital windows shook as mighty winds whistled past. Suddenly, the lights went out prompting the generators to come on. Mama kept insisting we go home to be with her granddaughters.

Her voice weak. She looked up at John and whispered," I think this is it, I'm on my way out." John was silent. My heart sank. I feared she was right. We both leaned down and kissed Mama on the cheek before leaving. I told her I would see her tomorrow, unaware what tomorrow may bring. I cried all the way back to Durham.

That was to be the last time I saw Mama alert and aware of her surroundings.

The following day, Hurricane Gloria began subsiding. John went to work and our oldest daughter went to school. Our younger daughter stayed with her other grandmother. I drove to Maine Medical Center in Portland to see Mama. Upon my arrival, I was told Mama had been moved to the intensive care unit. She was in a coma. The doctors took me aside and explained the diagnosis. Evidently, on the day Mama had visited Verda and had her near miss accident, she had suffered a heart attack. Since women experience different symptoms than men, Mama had thought it was the flu or severe indigestion. The muscle aches on her right and back sides were from the heart attack. Mama's heart had begun erratically flinging blood clots to her brain and leg.

This was why she kept repeating statements and seemed confused with garbled speech. The doctors believed the days she felt sick were when the blood clots were tossed through her body. The blood clots stopped the circulation in her leg. Back at the Parview hospital, one doctor had suggested amputation upon seeing her dark leg. The procedure would have been futile.

Mama's major body organs were now shutting down. Her kidneys were failing and her heart struggled to stay beating. Walking into the ICU seeing Mama's condition caused me great anguish. Tubes were everywhere.

Various machines projecting sounds I had never heard. Intravenous tubes sustaining her body, tubes pushing oxygen into her lungs and tubes connected to her kidneys expelling bodily fluids. All those tubes and machines were trying to keep Mama alive.

The following days were a blur. It felt like I was lost in a fog with no way out. Each day I stood by Mama's bedside listening to unfamiliar sounds. The constant beeping of the heart monitor, the respirator's swishing sound and the dripping of fluids from her catheter. In her deep comatose state, Mama looked helpless. My mind wandered back to happier childhood memories. Mama had been fiercely independent. She had owned and operated her own business. Raised me as a single mother. Renovated an old garage into a loving home. Mama had expressed many times she did not need a husband or partner.

There was one exception to that rule. Mama loved to dance. At a relative's wedding reception she once remarked to me, " Only when I dance, do I miss your father." The statement upset me when I first heard her say it. Did she not miss my father at all ? Since his death, Mama had mentioned his sense of humor and she would tell me how much he loved me.

Realistically, I knew what Mama meant in her confession statement. Mama enjoyed doing what she wanted, when she wanted without ever having to ask permission. She had never wanted to answer to anyone else.

On October 6, 1985 at the age of 64 years old, Mildred Louise Craig Henderson died. The death certificate states causes of death were multiple arterial emboli and renal failure. Mama's kidneys failed and her heart stopped. The heart attack emitted blood clots throughout her entire body. Smoking certainly attributed to my mother's death. She became one of the 250,000 women each year who die from heart disease. One out of five women who suffer heart attacks never survive. Those fleeting 3 weeks or exactly 22 days from her first symptoms were all too brief. Had she stopped smoking, had regular physical checkups and exercised more kept her alive longer ? Perhaps. None of these answers lessen the pain of losing my mother. What it does do for me is encourage a healthy lifestyle. It inspires me to " live each day like it is your last, because it just might be," a quote she told me my father would often say.

Tragically, five months after my mother's passing, John's mother succumbed to a sudden massive heart attack. A former smoker, she had stopped the day my first daughter was born. Losing these women deprived my daughters of knowing their grandmothers and sharing the special experience only grandmothers can provide.

For twenty-five years Nana loved me, and guided me. For 31 years Mama kept me safe, shaped my path and loved me unconditionally. Although their lives ended much sooner than I had hoped, I feel blessed for having them in my life.

Too distraught to tell my girls their beloved Nana had died, John offered to carry out the difficult task. Sadly five months later, it became my duty to tell them their Grandma had joined their Nana in heaven. We gathered both times for a heartbreaking cry together. My religious beliefs tell me Mama was united with her much loved father and mother. Reunited again with her sister Idolyne. Sometimes I close my eyes and see Tup and Mildred happily dancing together for eternity. Three months after Mama's death, my youngest daughter was born.

We brought her home from the hospital dressed in the yellow and white crocheted baby set her Nana had made for her. She was given the middle name of Mildred, which means " gentle strength." Mama would have liked that. Each one of these women Amanda Bean, Mildred Mcintosh, Lula Craig and Mildred Henderson created and shaped their own paths amidst lives filled with obstacles. Most refused to sidestep the problems that beseeched them.

Instead of giving up, they held family close while pushing past fears and apprehensions. No, they were not perfect people. Yes, mistakes were made. Hopefully, I learned from their mistakes, and have been inspired by their courage and will continue to feel blessed to be part of their heritage.

EPILOGUE

LOSING my mother was the hardest experiences I have ever known. She had been the stability and permanence in my life since birth. Unfortunately, she neglected her own health, all those years, to ensure mine. The culmination of various dynamics in Mama's life resulted in her death. A family history of heart disease. Smoking since the age of 14. A diet high in fatty foods and no exercise. These plus the fact that for over 31 years since my birth she refused to see a doctor.

Each matriarch who had their lives shaped by circumstances beyond their control or life changes they chose for themselves, resulted in who I am. My purpose for telling their stories is to inspire and validate other women who have struggled themselves.

Whether the setting is a small mill town in the Northeast or a farming community in the Midwest we all strive to make our lives and the lives of our families the best we can. With the means we have available. Faith and determination helped Gram, Nana and Mama cope when faced with misfortunes and tragedies. I may not agree with some of their decisions or the paths they followed but I will always admire their spirit......

GALLERY